SHE STOOPS TO CONQUER
BY OLIVER GOLDSMITH

MACMILLAN MASTER GUIDES

General Editor: James Gibson

Published:

JANE AUSTEN: **PRIDE AND PREJUDICE** Raymond Wilson

EMMA Norman Page

MANSFIELD PARK Richard Wirdnam

ROBERT BOLT: **A MAN FOR ALL SEASONS** Leonard Smith

EMILY BRONTË: **WUTHERING HEIGHTS** Hilda D. Spear

GEOFFREY CHAUCER: **THE PROLOGUE TO THE CANTERBURY TALES** Nigel Thomas and Richard Swan

CHARLES DICKENS: **GREAT EXPECTATIONS** Dennis Butts

HARD TIMES Norman Page

GEORGE ELIOT: **MIDDLEMARCH** Graham Handley

SILAS MARNER Graham Handley

OLIVER GOLDSMITH: **SHE STOOPS TO CONQUER** Paul Ranger

THOMAS HARDY: **FAR FROM THE MADDING CROWD** Colin Temblett-Wood

CHRISTOPHER MARLOWE: **DOCTOR FAUSTUS** David A. Male

GEORGE ORWELL: **ANIMAL FARM** Jean Armstrong

WILLIAM SHAKESPEARE: **MACBETH** David Elloway

A MIDSUMMER NIGHT'S DREAM Kenneth Pickering

ROMEO AND JULIET Helen Morris

THE WINTER'S TALE Diana Devlin

Forthcoming:

GEOFFREY CHAUCER: **THE MILLER'S TALE** Michael Alexander

T. S. ELIOT: **MURDER IN THE CATHEDRAL** Paul Lapworth

E. M. FORSTER: **A PASSAGE TO INDIA** Hilda D. Spear

WILLIAM GOLDING: **THE SPIRE** Rosemary Sumner

THOMAS HARDY: **TESS OF THE D'URBERVILLES** James Gibson

HARPER LEE: **TO KILL A MOCKINGBIRD** Jean Armstrong

THE METAPHYSICAL POETS Joan van Emden

ARTHUR MILLER: **THE CRUCIBLE** Leonard Smith

GEORGE BERNARD SHAW **ST JOAN** Leonee Ormond

WILLIAM SHAKESPEARE: **HAMLET** Jean Brooks

HENRY IV PART ONE Helen Morris

JULIUS CAESAR David Elloway

KING LEAR Francis Casey

OTHELLO Christopher Beddowes

TWELFTH NIGHT Edward Leeson

RICHARD SHERIDAN: **THE RIVALS** Jeremy Rowe

THE SCHOOL FOR SCANDAL Paul Ranger

JOHN WEBSTER: **THE DUCHESS OF MALFI/THE WHITE DEVIL** David A. Male

Also published by Macmillan

MACMILLAN MASTER SERIES

Mastering English Literature R. Gill
Mastering English Language S. H. Burton
Mastering English Grammar S. H. Burton

MACMILLAN MASTER GUIDES
SHE STOOPS TO CONQUER
BY OLIVER GOLDSMITH

PAUL RANGER

MACMILLAN

First edition 1985

Published by
MACMILLAN EDUCATION LTD
Houndmills, Basingstoke, Hampshire RG21 2XS
and London
Companies and representatives
throughout the world

Printed in Hong Kong

British Library Cataloguing in Publication Data
Ranger, Paul
She stoops to conquer by Oliver Goldsmith.—
(Macmillan master guides)
1. Goldsmith, Oliver. She stoops to conquer
I. Title   II. Goldsmith, Oliver. She stoops
to conquer
822'.6   PR3488
ISBN 0-333-38362-1   Pbk
ISBN 0-333-39469-0   Pbk export

CONTENTS

GENERAL EDITOR'S PREFACE

The aim of the Macmillan Master Guides is to help you to appreciate the book you are studying by providing information about it and by suggesting ways of reading and thinking about it which will lead to a fuller understanding. The section on the writer's life and background has been designed to illustrate those aspects of the writer's life which have influenced the work, and to place it in its personal and literary context. The summaries and critical commentary are of special importance in that each brief summary of the action is followed by an examination of the significant critical points. The space which might have been given to repetitive explanatory notes has been devoted to a detailed analysis of the kind of passage which might confront you in an examination. Literary criticism is concerned with both the broader aspects of the work being studied and with its detail. The ideas which meet us in reading a great work of literature, and their relevance to us today, are an essential part of our study, and our Guides look at the thought of their subject in some detail. But just as essential is the craft with which the writer has constructed his work of art, and this is considered under several technical headings – characterisation, language, style and stagecraft.

The authors of these Guides are all teachers and writers of wide experience, and they have chosen to write about books they admire and know well in the belief that they can communicate their admiration to you. But you yourself must read and know intimately the book you are studying. No one can do that for you. You should see this book as a lamp-post. Use it to shed light, not to lean against. If you know your text and know what it is saying about life, and how it says it, then you will enjoy it, and there is no better way of passing an examination in literature.

JAMES GIBSON

Cover illustration: *She Stoops to Conquer* by Thomas Parkinson.
© Robertson Davies Collection.

1 THE THEATRICAL CONTEXT

1.1   THE EIGHTEENTH-CENTURY PATENT HOUSES

The Auditorium

Oliver Goldsmith's sparkling comedy *She Stoops to Conquer* was first performed at the Theatre Royal at Covent Garden in 1773. This theatre stood on the site of the present Royal Opera House. The Theatre Royal was one of two 'patent houses' – theatres founded with royal permission – which regularly presented plays and musicals in the eighteenth century; its corresponding rival was the Theatre Royal in nearby Drury Lane.

The theatrical conditions in which the first season of the play was held were somewhat different from those of today, and it will be helpful in studying the play to be able to visualise its performance in an eighteenth-century theatre.

On going into the building the impression would be one of overcrowding compared with today's theatres. The foyer was no more than a corridor and the staircases were narrow and dark. Once in the auditorium the lack of space was accentuated. The house was divided into a number of clearly defined areas. At ground level was the pit, consisting of a series of twelve rows of backless benches, stepped in order to help visibility. A row of boxes surrounded the pit. Again, only benches were provided for the audience to sit on. Further tiers of boxes rose at the sides of the auditorium. As the overall layout of this was fan-shaped, it must have been difficult to see the whole of the stage from these positions. Above the rear boxes two galleries offered accommodation: the first of these was the Two Shilling Gallery (in coinage a modern ten penny piece is the equivalent of a two shilling piece, sometimes called a florin, although its purchasing power was much greater in the eighteenth century) and the second was the Shilling Gallery. At the front of the auditorium was a sunken area for the orchestra, an important feature in eighteenth-century performance. The whole of this area of the theatre was lit by candles held in a chandelier which was suspended from a central point of the domed ceiling. Additional candles burnt in the boxes and some were fitted to the front panels of these. They remained alight throughout the performance.

The Stage

A Georgian stage differs from a modern one in as much as it was divided into two areas: an acting area, and an area in which the scenery was set up. Jutting forward into the auditorium was the acting area known as the proscenium; this was simply a large, empty, apron stage. At either side of the stage at Covent Garden was a royal box and its occupants sat at stage level; not only were they in full view of the audience, they were also remarkably near the action of the play. Beyond the stage boxes were the proscenium doors, one on either side of the stage. Through these the actors made the majority of their entrances and exits, on their first appearance acknowledging the audience with a bow or curtsey. Immediately beyond the proscenium door was the proscenium arch, an elaborately decorated architectural feature which separated the scenic area from the rest of the theatre. It was from the proscenium arch that the green stage curtains were suspended and raised in swags at the beginning of the play, staying raised until the piece terminated. Thus any changes of scene were made openly with the audience watching. Now we come to the scenic area of the stage. Scenes were very much like those depicted in a Pollock toy theatre, consisting of a number of wing pieces at the sides of the stage and a pair of shutters which terminated the vista at the rear. On these would be painted the interior of Hardcastle's house. Even the furniture was painted on the scenes, and it was only if a functional chair or table was required that one of the Theatre Royal's liveried footmen would carry the furniture on to the stage. The brief scenes in 'The Three Pigeons' and at the bottom of Hardcastle's garden would be painted on screens which would be pushed across the front part of the scenes area.

A drawing made of the stage of the theatre in Covent Garden during a riot in 1763 shows how the stage was illuminated. The actors are lit by four hoops of candles and a central chandelier suspended above the proscenium; additional candles are fixed to panels beside the stage boxes. The scenery was lit by candles placed at the side of the wings and the screens; this meant that the scenes area was a somewhat dark place. A stage direction in the final scene of the play instructs Marlow and Kate Hardcastle to *retire . . . to the back scene*. Although unconcealed, the general gloom would prevent them appearing too obviously to the other characters on stage. Similar circumstances pertain when Sir Charles Marlow and Hardcastle hide behind a screen upstage. This particular term 'upstage' is used as the deck of the stage sloped upwards as it receded from the audience.

1.2 THE PAGE ON THE STAGE

The Introductory Scene

We can take the first act of *She Stoops to Conquer* and relate the conventions outlined above to the text. The play begins with a prologue which was spoken by the actor Edward Woodward. He would enter through one of the proscenium doors and speak his piece in front of the green curtain, the better to be seen and heard, standing at the front of the stage. After the speaker's exit through the proscenium door the heavy green curtain would be gathered upwards and the interior of the Hardcastles' house comes into view. If Hardcastle is to sit in his favourite chair (the one to which Lumpkin fastened his wig and which later Marlow commandeered) then the chair stands on the stage. Mr and Mrs Hardcastle enter through one of the proscenium doors – both come in by the same one as they are engaged in conversation – make their way to the front of the stage, and acknowledge the audience with a bow and a curtsey; then their dialogue as printed begins. Tony, on his entry, walks from one proscenium door, across the front of the stage, and makes for the other door: thus it is in this scene that one door represents the way to further rooms in the house, whilst the other leads to the front door. He is momentarily interrupted by his mother before leaving.

Hardcastle is left alone on the stage with a short, informative speech to give to the audience. As with the prologue he probably comes to the front of the stage and addresses the house directly. Each in turn, Kate Hardcastle and Constance Neville enter from the door that leads to the rest of the house. When the two young women play their scene together they may use a movement pattern which was common in comedy. On each speech the performer would cross the proscenium on the diagonal, so that the effect is of actresses playing a game of shuttlecock or badminton. As the proscenium at Covent Garden was over thirty feet wide this entailed a considerable degree of movement as well as careful timing in order to co-ordinate the speaking and the travel. However, this did give a liveliness to the dialogue as retorts flew backwards and forwards. At the end of this parry and thrust the two young women would leave the stage by the proscenium door.

The Scene in 'The Three Pigeons'

The scene changes from the house to the interior of 'The Three Pigeons'. One of the theatre's servants would remove Hardcastle's chair from the stage and others would bring in the alehouse table and a number of stools. As this was being done carpenters would push on to the scenic area screens on which a representation of the tavern was painted. If these were well downstage this would diminish the total depth. This flurry of activity would be initiated by the prompter, who sat in the wings in a hooded, leather armchair, blowing on a whistle. A well regulated stage crew would take only a matter of seconds to change the setting and its furnishings. As the change progressed Lumpkin and his drinking fellows would enter through one of the proscenium doors shouting their hurrahs which are given as the first line of the scene. As an accompaniment to the changes the orchestra usually played a few suitable bars of music, and it may be conjectured that the music was a snatch from the song which Lumpkin sings at the beginning of the scene.

The indication that the drinkers are seated around a table suggests that the first section of this scene is a sedentary one, although Lumpkin may sing his song standing on a bench, or even on the table. From one of the proscenium doors the landlord enters to announce the arrival of Hastings and Marlow. When the drinkers leave the stage there is a possibility that they do so through a door in the back-scene. Marlow and

Hastings, of course, enter by the proscenium door through which the Landlord made his first appearance, and their exit, back into the open air, is by the same way. This, then, only leaves the stage-hands to remove the alehouse furnishings and the carpenters to retract the screens so that the scenic area may be restored to Hardcastle's house. It is to be emphasised that each of these changes was seen by the audience, and possibly formed an interesting adjunct to the action of the play.

Acting Styles

A slight indication of the acting styles employed in this play is given in a painting by Thomas Parkinson. It depicts the garden scene in Act 5. The actors are arranged in a line across the front of the stage. Hardcastle stands squarely facing the audience; his wife, mistaking him for a highwayman, has dropped to her knees and tugs at his clothes as she begs for pity. From the painting it is obvious that at this moment Tony Lumpkin is addressing the house. He stands to one side of his parents, pointing to them with both hands as if he has no part in the scene, but instead is there to demonstrate to the audience the plight his mother is in. This is an important consideration: often characters speak directly to the audience; additionally, much of the acting is directed deliberately towards the audience instead of between characters. There is a greater sense of sharing the play with the spectators than in the performance of a modern piece.

1.3 STAGING AS A STUDY METHOD

Motivation

She Stoops to Conquer was not written as a text to be read, but as a play to be acted, and those who study the comedy will find it advantageous to rehearse sections of each act as a study method. It is, of course, necessary to bear in mind the description of the theatrical conditions given above. From performed excerpts it should be possible to learn about the following points: the underlying motivations for the character's words (this is sometimes referred to as 'sub-text'); the relationship of the characters on the stage at a given time; and the devices that Goldsmith uses to give information and to advance the plot. An example will help to make this clear. Let us take for this the exchange between Hardcastle and Kate in the first scene of the play.

Motivation is a complex issue here. Some of the time Hardcastle is simply giving Kate, and thereby the audience, information: Marlow will arrive that evening; he is a scholarly man destined for public service; what is more, he is thoroughly presentable. Kate's responses are on two levels. At first they are highly artificial: it is a convention that she should be compliant with her father's wishes as it has already been established she is the dutiful daughter; but secondarily, in responding to the news of Marlow's handsome appearance, a vivacious enthusiasm takes over. This is immediately tempered by Hardcastle's remark, cunningly presented as an after-thought, that Marlow is extraordinarily reserved. An artificial dialogue takes over as Kate and Hardcastle speak to each other in such catchphrases as '. . . a reserved lover . . . always makes a suspicious husband'.

Relationships

The relationship of one character to another is revealed in the dialogue which passes between them. It is more strikingly demonstrated in the visual and physical relationship that they adopt to each other on stage. The actors will need to ask themselves such questions as: does Hardcastle sit in his chair to give Kate the news about Marlow's visit? or does he more formally give this standing? Kate comes near her father to kiss his hand. When does she first advance towards him? And for how long does she remain in proximity? This nearness to each other signifies a fondness between father and daughter.

One of the devices used for establishing the dutifulness of Kate is Goldsmith's simple touch of showing the girl wearing her elaborate day dress at the beginning of the excerpt, so allowing her to rehearse to Hardcastle their agreement that she will wear simple clothes in the evening. Kate's compliance with Hardcastle's wishes about the visit of the man he intends as her husband follows naturally from this. Much information is given to the audience in this short excerpt – most of it very naturally through conversation. We learn of the agreement relating to the dresses; who Marlow is and what his characteristics are; we also learn something of Kate's philosophical outlook and determination, in her speech before her father's exit. A further method of imparting information, and a much used one in the theatre, is the letter from the outside world giving news of Marlow's impending visit. Another letter is used later in the play – the note from Hastings, intercepted by Mrs Hardcastle, which appears to frustrate the planned action. In reality it advances the plot.

Performing short excerpts from the play, and combining each performance with a careful analysis, will help to establish for the student such points as those itemised above. The words of the playwright are a groundplan for informed experimentation. Throughout this process of practical study the participants must attempt to be faithful to the intentions of Oliver Goldsmith and bear in mind the dramatic conventions of his day.

2 OLIVER GOLDSMITH: LIFE AND BACKGROUND

2.1 YOUTHFUL DAYS

> ... we lived several years in a state of much happiness; not but that
> we sometimes had those little rubs which Providence sends to enhance
> the value of its favours. My orchard was often robbed by schoolboys,
> and my wife's custards plundered by the cats or the children. The
> Squire would sometimes fall asleep in the most pathetic parts of my
> sermon, or his lady return my wife's civilities at church with a
> mutilated curtsey. But we soon got over the uneasiness caused by
> these accidents ...

This vignette from Oliver Goldsmith's novel *The Vicar of Wakefield*
may be a mirror-image of the world in which the infant Oliver grew up.
He was born on 10 November 1728 near Ballymohan in Ireland. His
father was a Church of Ireland clergyman whose personal traits were
lovingly drawn in the novel in the character of Dr Primrose. As a child
Goldsmith was surrounded by storytellers: there were the Irish ballad
singers, a blind harper named O'Carolan, and the family's old dairymaid.
This company augured well for the future playwright and novelist.

After a few years the family moved to Lissoy where Goldsmith grew
to adolescence. When Goldsmith was a teenager an incident occurred
which as a writer he was to use towards the end of his life. His sister,
Mrs Hodson, records it in a manuscript which outlined a few of the
events of Goldsmith's life. On a journey from Edgeworthstown back to
his home the young lad was loitering, looking at the large country
houses on the way. He came to a village called Ardagh and realised that

darkness would fall before he reached home. He possessed unaccustomed wealth – a guinea, given to him before the journey by a friend. Goldsmith enquired of a passer-by the way to the best inn in the district. The man whom he addressed was a wag, a fencing master named Cornelius Kelly. Immediately the boy was taken to the house of Squire Featherstone and this was pointed out to him as the inn. He was well feasted by the Squire, bought the Squire's daughter bottles of wine, and when shown to his bedroom ordered a hot cake for breakfast the next morning. It wasn't until he attempted to settle his account that the good-natured Squire, realising the deception from the first, as did his wife and daughter, let Goldsmith know that he was a friend of his father, Squire of Ardagh, and no innkeeper. This adventure Goldsmith used nearly thirty years later as the basis of the plot of *She Stoops to Conquer*. Ardagh House still stands, although it is now a convent.

The family was somewhat feckless in money matters and consequently was unable to send Goldsmith to Trinity College, Dublin as an undergraduate. Instead he sat for a scholarship examination and entered the college in 1745 as a sizar. This meant that board and education were given in return for Goldsmith performing a number of menial tasks such as helping with the cleaning. To look at, Goldsmith was an ugly youth, as his face was badly scarred by smallpox. His behaviour tended to rowdiness. On one occasion he joined with some fellows in ducking a bailiff. Poverty dogged him, as it was to throughout his life. However, Goldsmith mastered the art of composing ballads, which he sold to a printer for five shillings each. Money burnt holes in his pockets, and just as he had attempted to rapidly spend the gift of a guinea, so the payments for his poetry were spent in entertainment and gambling. In an impulsive gesture he gave all of his blankets to a beggarwoman and her children. It was at this stage in his life that, like Marlow, he became acquainted with 'idle women' at riotous parties. Whilst he was at college his father died, leaving a much impoverished family.

Goldsmith graduated in 1749 and spent three years at home. These were profligate days, and as well as shades of Marlow we can also see the forerunner of Tony Lumpkin in the young Irishman who gambled, hunted, played cards and frequented the tavern. The bishop was surprised by a visit from Goldsmith wearing scarlet breeches: he had come to enquire about ordination. He was rejected. He gave the law a trial, but when a cardsharper gained all of his money Goldsmith returned home again. At teaching he was a failure.

Church, law and school had attracted him, but in none had he found fulfilment. In 1752 he went to the harsher climate of Edinburgh to study medicine, and that grey city was soon surprised to count among its inhabitants a young man who sported silver hat-lace, white fustian and claret-coloured cloth. Here again, there may well be an image of Marlow. Travels abroad took him to Holland, the Low Countries, France, Germany, Switzerland and Italy. He had undertaken the Grand Tour, albeit an impoverished version. Nevertheless, those who went on the tour tended to return to England as 'men of sentiment' shaped by emotional encounters such as one's first sight of the Alps, or of the ruins of ancient Rome which spoke of the brevity of human life and invited their spectator to indulge in melancholy, an emotion which, it was thought, cleansed a man's heart and mind.

Experiences such as these gave their recipients a greater emotional response not only to natural and historical phenomena; they also heightened numbers of everyday encounters. Here is an echo of Marlow, the man whose equilibrium can become upset at the sight of Kate Hardcastle, the strongly virtuous young woman destined to be his wife.

2.2 GOLDSMITH THE WRITER

The Citizen of the World

On his return Goldsmith, having no desire to live in Ireland, set up in London. He attempted several jobs (teaching again, proof-reading, apothecary's assistant) until by 1759 he was fully employed as a writer. The following year he was invited by John Newbery to submit a series of articles for a daily newspaper, the *Public Ledger*. This was in the format of a number of letters ostensibly written by a Chinese philosopher visiting eighteenth-century England. Through this device Goldsmith was enabled to take a distanced stand and comment critically, usually by means of satire and irony, on the customs of the day. For students of *She Stoops to Conquer* the letter entitled 'The Chinese goes to see a play' is of special interest, for it paints a picture of the theatre that Goldsmith knew. He describes the audience sitting in the various parts of the auditorium. In the boxes were the wealthy who visited the playhouse as much to be seen as to see:

I could not avoid considering them as acting parts in a dumb shew, not a curtsey or nod, that was not the result of art; not a look nor a smile that was not designed for murder.

In the pit sat those who 'seemed to consider themselves as judges of the merit of the poet and the performers', although Goldsmith challenged that supposition, aware that 'not one in an hundred of them knew even the first principles of criticism'. Waiting for the entertainment to begin the Chinaman observed that the audience passed the time eating oranges, or reading the text of the play or in making assignations. Soon the atmosphere of the crowded playhouse gripped the writer and he found that

the lights, the music, the ladies in their gayest dresses, the men with cheerfulness and expectation in their looks, all conspired to make a most agreeable picture, and to fill an heart that sympathises at human happiness with inexpressible serenity.

The last two paragraphs of the Chinaman's letter pass from description to philosophical considerations and help us to realise why it was that Goldsmith eventually wrote comedies rather than the more prestigious tragedies. The Chinaman had been to see a tragedy, possibly *Douglas*, and he found that for himself it was impossible to sympathise with the plight of the characters through five acts: 'pity is but a short lived passion'. The actors' constant tones of despair were wearisome and theatrically ineffective. As the years went by Goldsmith became convinced that there was a place on the English stage for genuine humour of the kind that he witnessed in the comedies of William Shakespeare (1564-1616) and of George Farquhar (1678-1707). In these a sunny pastoralism reflected the traditional joys of country life and the knockabout humour of rustic characters led to genuine belly laughs amongst the audience.

Recognition

By the early 1760s Goldsmith began to be recognised as a writer. Several of the well-known personages of the day took him up, with the result that he became acquainted with London's literary circle. He became a close friend of the large and irrepressibly witty Dr Samuel

Johnson (1709-84). It was to Johnson that Goldsmith, as a mark of his gratitude for that gentleman's encouragement of his literary work, dedicated *She Stoops to Conquer*. In turn Johnson introduced Goldsmith to Sir Joshua Reynolds (1723-92), one of the foremost portrait painters of the eighteenth century. When the Royal Academy was founded Reynolds invited Goldsmith to become the Historian of the institution, a not unsuitable post as the writer was prolific in producing such surveys as *The History of the Earth and Animated Nature*.

Reynolds took to Goldsmith and wrote an autobiographical sketch of him in which we see not only the man himself, but also gain a glimpse of the origins within the writer of some of his own characters. His behaviour in polite society was gauche: fearful of being neglected he drew attention to himself by suddenly breaking into song, dancing, or even by standing on his head. When he was engaged in conversation it tended to be loud. Reynolds put this down to Goldsmith's late entry into London society:

> He had lived a great part of his life with mean people. All his old habits were against him. It was too late to learn new ones, or at least for the new to sit easy upon him.

In this he resembled Marlow, who found company, at least that of polite women, difficult to cope with. And one can recognise here too, the origins of the noisily rumbustious Tony Lumpkin. In 1770 Reynolds painted the portrait of Goldsmith which is now in the National Portrait Gallery. It was not, remarked an admirer, the man who was seen in daily life: instead, in its lack of formality, for Goldsmith had taken off his wig and cravat, it presented the viewer with a picture of an unpretentious, and still somewhat ugly, person.

We can see elements of Goldsmith's own biography in his writings. *The Vicar of Wakefield*, in part a picture of his childhood home, was published in 1766. It was Dr Johnson who arranged for the sale of the manuscript to the printer John Newbery at a time when his friend was in danger of being evicted from his lodging for failing to pay his rent. Johnson related the story:

> He . . . told me that he had a novel ready for the press, which he produced to me. I looked into it and saw its merit; told the landlady I should soon return, and having gone to a bookseller, sold it for

sixty pounds. I brought Goldsmith the money, and he discharged his rent, not without rating his landlady in a high tone for having used him so ill.

The Deserted Village

We can also see Goldsmith's love of both English and Irish rural life in his works. It is against this background that *She Stoops to Conquer* is enacted and, of course, it is the backdrop to *The Vicar of Wakefield*. Goldsmith's greatest poetic tribute to the English countryside is *The Deserted Village* which was published in 1770 and established his reputation as a poet. Two contemporary issues prompted the writing. From 1760 vast tracts of common land were being enclosed and villagers who had reared animals on these were deprived of a source of livelihood. From the previous decade some of the wealthy landowners had demolished whole villages in order to extend and reshape the parks surrounding their houses: even the Hardcastles are in the process of making 'improvements'. Perhaps in writing *The Deserted Village* Goldsmith had in mind the first Earl of Harcourt who removed the medieval village of Nuneham in Oxfordshire which stood in the way of his picturesque garden:

> Thus fares the land by luxury betrayed . . .
> The mournful peasant leads his humble band
> And while he sinks, without one arm to save,
> The country blooms – a garden and a grave.

The Good Natur'd Man

Goldsmith's first play, *The Good Natur'd Man* was completed in 1767 and staged in the following year at the Theatre Royal, Covent Garden. His piece reflected two aspects of life, 'nature and humour'. Unfortunately it was on these two counts that critics attacked *The Good Natur'd Man*. The play was constructed around the adventures of Honeywood, an open-hearted young man whose good nature is expended to a foolish degree. By this device the playwright was suggesting that an excess of virtue is, in itself, a vice. Such a proposition was at odds with the sensibility of most of the members of the audience, for Goldsmith was determined to avoid the serious moralising of many of the sentimental comedies of his day. In them heroes and heroines were presented as highly idealised characters. Honeywood represents the gullible folly that may be found in the natural world. But Goldsmith not only gave his audience an unheroic hero, he also depicted aspects of low life which grievously offended his critics. One such scene occurred in the third act in which a coarse bailiff arrived to arrest Honeywood for debt. Perhaps it was the same critics who were to be offended later by the gallants at 'The Three Pigeons'.

The play ran for only eleven nights, although Goldsmith made £400 from the piece. What was galling was the successful run simultaneously of a new sentimental comedy by Hugh Kelly (1739-77), *False Delicacy*, at the Theatre Royal, Drury Lane. A deft construction of plot was a feature of many sentimental dramas and this Goldsmith lacked in his first essay for the theatre. He learned rapidly, however, by his clumsy mistakes, and five years later, in writing *She Stoops to Conquer* he had overcome the initial difficulties he found in plotting and narration.

The 'laughing comedy'

A matter of weeks before *She Stoops to Conquer* was staged an article by Goldsmith appeared in the *Westminster Magazine*. Entitled 'An Essay on the Theatre' it was a lengthy comparison of 'laughing comedy' (a form of comedy to which Goldsmith's work corresponded) with sentimental comedy, the then prevailing genre, to which the writer referred as a 'species of Bastard Tragedy'. The essay was a plea that humour might once more pervade the comedies staged in the theatre. Considerable stir was caused by Goldsmith's argument. It was this that generated interest in anticipation of his comedy *She Stoops to Conquer*, which opened at the Theatre Royal, Covent Garden in March 1773.

2.3 DEMISE AND REMEMBRANCE

For fifteen years Goldsmith had laboured against the clock to produce enough writing to enable him to survive. His generosity to his friends and to the bevy of hangers-on, together with his own lack of skill in managing his financial affairs, prevented him from leading more than a hand-to-mouth existence. He began to suffer the strain of overwork. For some months depression attacked him; he ate little and seemed to be suffering from a kidney disease. His friends noticed that he was no longer the noisy jester entertaining the company. Hoping that an escape from the commotion of London would do him good, Goldsmith spent a few months at Kingsbury. By March 1774 he was back in London, suffering from feverishness. His friends little realised the seriousness of his illness and were greatly shocked when, in April, he died following a series of convulsions. They buried him in the Temple Church in the City of London, and set up in Westminster Abbey a memorial dedicated to 'Olivarii Goldsmith, Poetae, Physici, Historici'.

His fame spread from England to his childhood home of Lissoy in Ireland. There the inn was repaired and appropriately named in memory of Goldsmith, and his creation, Tony Lumpkin, 'The Three Jolly Pigeons'. That is a mark of fame!

3 SUMMARIES
AND
CRITICAL COMMENTARY

3.1 SYNOPSIS

Sir Charles Marlow has proposed a match between his own son, Young Marlow, and Kate Hardcastle, the daughter of Squire Hardcastle who lives in a country village with his wife Dorothy and her son by a former marriage, Tony Lumpkin. Accordingly Marlow travels from town to meet Kate accompanied by his friend George Hastings who is in love with Kate's cousin Constance Neville, an orphan who resides with the Hardcastles. Marriage with Kate is difficult as Mrs Hardcastle has decided that in order to keep Constance's fortune (consisting mainly of jewellery) in the family she shall marry Tony; the two realise they are incompatible. It is Hastings' intention on this visit to elope with Constance, travel to the Continent and there marry her.

Nearing their goal the two travellers lose their way and seek direction at a noisy tavern, 'The Three Pigeons'. Lumpkin, realising who they are, misdirects them to his step-father's house, pretending it is an inn called 'The Buck's Head'. Much of the humour of the play consists of the traumas that arise from this mistaken identity. On meeting Kate for the first time Marlow reveals himself to be extremely bashful, so much so that he is unable to look at her, even. Thus we learn of his peculiar characteristics – shyness in the presence of young women of his own class, and a brazen boldness in meeting women of a lower social standing. In order to woo the young man, who, Kate feels, is promising material, she pretends to be a barmaid at the inn. To her in this guise Marlow shows the precocious side of his nature in a scene in which he attempts to make violent love to her.

Meanwhile Hastings and Constance suffer a number of difficulties as they prepare to elope, the chief of which is to obtain Constance's fortune. Mrs Hardcastle manages to intercept a note from Hastings to Lumpkin which apprises her of the arrangements for the flight. Instantly she prepares to take Constance to the house of her Aunt Pedigree, several hours' journey away, where it will be impossible for Hastings to see her. Lumpkin is to ride beside the carriage and direct the driver. Cunningly he takes the occupants of the coach on a circular route and brings them back safely to the garden of the Hardcastles where Hastings is stationed. Together the young lovers steal away, but without the fortune.

Marlow learns of his mistake in taking the house for an inn. Watched by a hidden Hardcastle and by his own father Sir Charles, he proposes to Kate, who by this time he mistakenly imagines to be a poor relation of the Hardcastle family. The two fathers appear from their hiding place and the many problems of identity are solved. At this auspicious point Hastings reappears with Constance; the pair have decided only to get married with Hardcastle's blessing so that they may obtain their rightful fortune. Lumpkin renounces any claim to Constance and the audience is left with the prospect of the two couples happily looking forward to their respective marriages.

3.2 SUMMARIES AND COMMENTARY

Prologue

The prologue to *She Stoops to Conquer* was written by David Garrick (1717–79), the manager of Covent Garden's rival patent house in Drury Lane. Garrick was one of the finest actors of his day, notable for introducing a naturalistic form of acting into his productions. He was a friend of Samuel Johnson, and it may be that Johnson was instrumental in persuading the actor to write this prologue. This would imply at least a commendation of the play – although Garrick was unwilling to stage it at Drury Lane!

The prologue was spoken by a comic actor, Edward Woodward, who turned down the role of Tony Lumpkin in the play, suspecting that the piece would be a failure. He is dressed in black, in mourning for the 'Comic muse' who lies dying.

The gist of the argument is that the true 'laughing comedy' which gives amusement to audiences is dying and is being replaced by 'sentimental comedy', a form of serious (in spite of being comedy), moralising drama which makes an emotional demand on spectators. If this type of comedy gains the stage completely then Woodward as well as Edward (Ned) Shuter (who played the part of Hardcastle) will be out of work. Woodward makes an attempt at imitating a sentimental actor performing a few lines from a sentimental comedy – but realises that this heavy moralising will not do for him. The lines, in fact, are not from a play but from *The Hind and the Panther*, a religious, satirical poem by John Dryden (1631–1700), a revered Augustan writer.

At the end of the prologue the Speaker makes the point that a doctor, that is Dr Oliver Goldsmith, has come to restore his ailing patient, comedy, and with five drafts, or potions, corresponding to the five acts of the play, he will reinfuse comedy with lively and amusing situations.

The prologue is presented in the form of an extended metaphor: true comedy is the patient dying of sentimentalism; Goldsmith is the physician who will restore her; and the audience will decide whether he is a 'regular' (qualified) doctor or a 'quack' – a word which suggests an amateur with hints of charlatanism.

Audiences regarded both the prologue and the epilogue as important comments on the play: there were occasions in which minor riots ensued when either was omitted. The prologue was a valuable opportunity to enlarge on the playwright's reasons for composing his drama. Usually the prologue was spoken in front of the green proscenium curtain by an actor. As he finished speaking the curtain would rise, revealing the first scene of the play.

This is a typical example of a prologue: it is written in rhyming couplets of iambic pentameters (a metrical beat of five strong stresses to a line) and is of the expected length. It is usual for a performer in the play to speak the prologue; however in this instance the convention was abandoned.

Act 1, Scene 1

Summary

In the first scene of his comedy Goldsmith establishes three things: the principal characters of the play, the location in which the characters perform the action of the piece and the circumstances which lead to the development of the plot.

Mr and Mrs Hardcastle are the first to enter. Goldsmith presents their contrasting natures economically. Hardcastle is a traditionalist – he loves 'old times, old manners, old books and old wine'. We soon discover that he has a daughter by a previous marriage, Kate, whom he treats in a kindly but firm manner, thereby living up to his name. His second wife, Dorothy Hardcastle, however, has an interest in London society (her first speech expresses a longing for a 'trip to town') and she takes a lively interest in the fashions of the day. To accommodate these she tries to lose a few years from her age. She has a son by her first marriage, Tony Lumpkin, who, she hopes, will eventually marry Constance.

The couple prepare for Tony Lumpkin's entry by discussing his characteristics: Mrs Hardcastle in soft terms speaks of the invalid boy, whilst Hardcastle itemises his pranks as 'burning the footman's shoes, frightening the maids, and worrying the kittens'. Mrs Hardcastle envisages some Latin tuition as a suitable form of schooling, perhaps suggesting his vocation is to be a clergyman or a lawyer; Hardcastle claims that stables and taverns are the only schools the lad will go to. On Lumpkin's entry we realise that Hardcastle's is the more realistic appraisal of the fellow's character. Tony Lumpkin lives up to his name – he seems to be a self-willed alehouse clod.

As Kate Hardcastle enters immediately after Lumpkin's exit we instinctively compare the two characters. She is polite in addressing both her father and stepmother; obedient in following Hardcastle's whim requiring her to wear a plain 'housewife's' dress in the evening, although, by arrangement, she wears a fashionable silk dress in order to pay calls and receive visitors earlier each day; and she is circumspectly interested when she hears that her father has invited Marlow, a young man whom he hopes she will marry, to stay for a while.

The final person to enter is Constance Neville, Mrs Hardcastle's niece, and the near friend of Kate. From Constance we learn that Marlow is an inseparable friend of Hastings, a young gentleman who admires her. Thus it is, in conversations towards the end of the scene, that the audience learns that there are two pairs of young people, Kate and Marlow, and Constance and Hastings. The audience is also given clues about the characteristics of Marlow well in advance of his entry. Hardcastle tells us that he is a bashful and reserved young man; Constance can give further information which Hardcastle does not know: when Marlow mixes with girls of low class he becomes a very different person.

Commentary

The scene takes place in 'an old fashioned House', one of Hardcastle's, rather than his wife's, choosing. She, indeed, complains that the building resembles an inn. 'Improvements' are being undertaken, but the exact nature of these is not stipulated. Possibly several of the rooms are being altered to the gothic style, or changes in the gardens may be in process in order to make them more picturesque. The prompting for this probably comes from Mrs Hardcastle as these would both be fashions of the day.

Although we see nothing of the surrounding countryside we hear about some of the neighbouring inhabitants. People of a comparable class with the Hardcastles sound, with the exception of Cripplegate the dancing master, to be truly rural: there are the Miss Hoggs, Mrs Grigsby (a grig is a grasshopper) and Mrs Oddfish. Tony Lumpkin's low class friends are given rustic names too, along with their occupations: Dick Muggins the exciseman (perhaps this suggests that Hardcastle's house is near the coast), Jack Slang the horse doctor, and Tom Twist.

In presenting this scene to the audience Oliver Goldsmith introduces nothing that is not used later in the development of the plot. The audience is prepared by Mrs Hardcastle's description for Marlow and Hastings to mistake the house for an inn and for Kate to be taken for a barmaid because of her plain wear in the evening. We are introduced to the theme of wealth, too. Tony Lumpkin has inherited an annuity from his father and Constance Neville owns a considerable quantity of jewellery which her aunt manages for her. The recovery of these jewels will add to the farcical nature of the plot later in the play. Even Tony Lumpkin's fleeting appearance helps to establish that he has little respect for his doting mother and will actively side against her when occasion demands.

Act 1, Scene 2

Summary

The cameo presented in the previous scene of Hardcastle and his wife at home is paralleled in this scene by the stage picture of Tony Lumpkin sitting at the head of the table in 'The Three Pigeons' very much at home. Shouting, singing and a muster of shabby fellows all help to make an aural and visual contrast with the preceding scene. In his song in honour of the alehouse Lumpkin dismisses schoolmasters and Methodist preachers, a break-away group of dissenters who preached a warm and enthusiastic faith which was in contrast with the Anglicanism which Parson Oddfish would have presented at the parish church. Needless to say, the Methodists were opposed to alehouses. The audience heard in the preceding scene of some of the frequenters of the tavern – in this scene rustics come into view. There is irony in the second fellow's remark that Lumpkin never sings of low life – the third verse is in praise of the low life at the alehouse. A little of Lumpkin's background is sketched in: it seems to be generally known that his father left him considerable wealth which he will inherit when he comes of age, at 21. Lumpkin is a living replica of his father – the squire who excels in country pursuits – and yet the picture of him is quite distinct from that of the rural but domesticated Hardcastle.

The Landlord announces that Marlow and Hastings are at the door – they have lost their way. Instantly Lumpkin hits on a plan to avenge his stepfather's constant grumbles about his behaviour; he will direct the travellers to Hardcastle's house pretending it is an inn called 'The Buck's Head'. This ploy forms the basis of the ensuing plot.

Remarks in the preceding scene have prepared the audience for this entry of Marlow and Hastings. Early in the exchange of words Marlow's 'unaccountable reserve' is commented on in order to reinforce the information previously given. Lumpkin's spirit of fantasy begins to work at once. In his own terms he describes Hardcastle and Kate in an unattractive light but presents himself as an 'agreeable youth'. More fantastic is the description of the surrounding countryside that he and the Landlord fabricate: an area of boggy roads, hills and dangerous commons. However, the way to 'The Buck's Head' is presented as an easy journey a mile up the road. A further invention is Lumpkin's notion that Hardcastle is an innkeeper on the verge of retirement aspiring to be recognised as one of the gentry. The deluded travellers make their way out.

Commentary

In this scene Goldsmith lays the basis for the plot. The mistakes of the night begin with Marlow and Hastings assuming that Hardcastle's house is 'The Buck's Head'. Thus he is building on the impression he carefully contrived earlier of the rambling old-fashioned mansion, and combining with this mistake facets of Hardcastle's and Kate's way of life which he has also carefully established.

Goldsmith also develops two senses of the countryside. There is the 'real' environment as it is presented to us in conversation, the old house on the hill, the nearby forest, the church, the alehouse on the edge of the village. But there is, too, an eighteenth-century 'caprice' or contrived landscape which exists only in the imagination of Lumpkin and the Landlord, a dangerous and fearsome countryside. To this Goldsmith returns in the fifth act of the play. This is one of the scenes in *She Stoops to Conquer* which drew a condemnation from some critics for Goldsmith's concern with low life characters in unsavoury environments. But the scene is a most effective foil to the previous one set in a country mansion in which, although there is a lack of fashionability and although, too, the servants are somewhat clumsy fellows, there is at least quiet orderliness and good living.

Act 2

Summary

The scene returns to Hardcastle's house in which the audience sees Hardcastle attempting, without any degree of success, to drill the servants in the method of waiting at table in preparation for the arrival of Hastings and Marlow. Again low life is portrayed in this section of the act; the gap between the expectations of polished behaviour and what the servants can manage adds humour to the piece. The servants, in their conversation, emphasise that Hardcastle is a great teller of military tales.

The scene is interrupted by the arrival of Hastings and Marlow. They both admire the house which, as Lumpkin intended, they take to be an inn. Indeed, it appears so hospitable that they fear the charges will be high. In conversation with Hastings we learn that Marlow has spent much of his life residing either at colleges or at inns, and it is this that has deprived him of mixing sociably with reputable ladies. On the rare occasions he has met a young lady of his own class she has petrified him. Marlow claims that he is visiting Hardcastle in order that Hastings may again meet Constance Neville.

Hardcastle greets his visitors with a phrase he is later to regret: This is Liberty-hall. He is immediately mistaken for the innkeeper. In no time two parallel conversations are taking place: whilst Marlow and

Hastings speak of the need to change from their travelling clothes into something finer, Hardcastle is launched on an anecdote about one of the Duke of Marlborough's campaigns. The visitors call for a cup of punch and then discuss the evening meal. Roger, one of the servants, brings in a bill of fare. The visitors are amazed at the quality and quantity of the proposed meal and Marlow delegates the choice of food to Hardcastle. He leaves the room in order to inspect his bedroom and check that the beds are aired, followed by Hardcastle protesting that this has been attended to.

Constance Neville discovers Hastings and, realising that he has mistaken the Hardcastles' house for an inn, at the prompting of her cousin Tony, quickly puts matters right. Hastings briefs Constance on his plot for their elopement: once the horses are refreshed he and Constance will travel to France. Constance is anxious to get her jewels from her aunt and so secure the fortune her uncle has left her. Together the lovers decide to leave Marlow in the deception that he is staying at an inn, in case he wishes to leave before their plan can be effected.

When Marlow returns from the bedroom Hastings tells him that Constance and Kate have arrived. He pretends that they need to renew their horses at the inn. Marlow, although anxious to leave in order to avoid meeting Kate, is persuaded to stay. A humorous conversation ensues between Marlow and Kate in which the young man is so overcome by shyness he is scarcely able to finish a phrase and Kate is left to frame his stutterings into sentences. Marlow does manage to get out that he has been an observer of life rather than a participant in it. Kate dubs him a 'man of sentiment', a serious, honourable and highly sensitive young man. Momentarily left alone on the stage Kate is able to sum up in a speech to the audience her impression of Marlow: 'He has good sense, but then so buried in his fears, that it fatigues one more than ignorance'. She determines to discover how she can 'teach him a little confidence'.

The fashions of London are the topics that Mrs Hardcastle and Hastings pursue as they re-enter the room. Unashamedly Hastings flatters Mrs Hardcastle on her hairstyle, her dress and her youthful appearance. Not realising Hasting's quest for Constance, Mrs Hardcastle coos over Tony's and Constance's 'little sports', finding similarities of face and height in the two young people which she sees as an auspicious sign of their suitability for each other. As is his wont though, Tony Lumpkin rapidly upsets his doting mother.

When Tony and Hastings are left alone together Tony attacks his cousin, calling her a 'bitter cantankerous toad'. Hastings offers to take Constance off Lumpkin's hands provided he helps the couple to elope. Not only does Tony promise to provide horses for the chaise, but also to try to extricate some of Constance's fortune from Mrs Hardcastle. This is the first point in the play in which Lumpkin's character has been presented in a friendly and agreeable light and Hastings rightly draws the attention of the audience to his virtues: '. . . this looks like a lad of spirit'.

Commentary

In this act the deception that Tony Lumpkin conceives is made to work: Marlow, and for a little while Hastings too, mistake Hardcastle's old mansion for an inn and treat Hardcastle himself as a common innkeeper. This mistaken identity allows for a number of ironic remarks to be made, the most obvious of which is Marlow's and Hastings' tendency to pick up Hardcastle's phrase, 'This is Liberty-hall' and to use it against the master of the house. There is, too, the added complicity on the part of Constance and Hastings, after discovering the trick played on Marlow, of allowing him to remain duped, as well as keeping the Hardcastles in ignorance of the mistake in identity.

It is noteworthy that the numbers of people who are fooled by Lumpkin's trick are diminishing. At first the travellers and the inhabitants of Hardcastle's house were involved. In this act Constance, Kate and Hastings have discovered the mistake in identity, leaving Mr and Mrs Hardcastle and Marlow with crossed wires. Throughout the complications, however, the members of the audience have known of the deception practised on all parties and so they can gain amusement from the complications that ensue.

The plot is advanced by the plan that Hastings makes of eloping with Constance. This is given further interest by his enlisting the help of Tony Lumpkin, and by Lumpkin's offer of attempting to retrieve the jewels belonging to Constance. There is, too, a hint of a development which will come to fruition in Act 3, in Kate's determination to help Marlow gain enough confidence to make a proposal to her.

We noted that in the previous act Goldsmith was describing both the world of the village in which the Hardcastles live and an antipathetic world that exists only as a fantasy. In this act the writer develops two more 'worlds'. There is Mrs Hardcastle's view of the world of fashionable metropolitan society. It is a highly subjective and imaginative view of a world which, to some extent, is a fabrication, although she claims it is partly based on information given in 'the Scandalous Magazine', possibly in reality a journal as proper as the *Town and Country Magazine* which contained reviews of books and plays as well as a social circular. The other 'world' is that of Hardcastle's campaigns in war. There are clues too, mistaken dates and places, for example, that this is at least a partly fabricated world. So both Mr and Mrs Hardcastle, as well as living in the reality of their rambling manor house on the edge of the village, inhabit worlds of the imagination which give a further dimension to their character.

Act 3

Summary
As the day has worn on, Kate changes her dress, and by this simple action she prepares the audience for a further mistaken identity. Hardcastle and his daughter compare notes on Marlow. To Hardcastle he appears a loud-mouthed, brazenly familiar young man who has interrupted the telling of one of the old campaigner's best anecdotes. In contrast Kate finds him timidly bashful and over-ready to excuse himself from her company. For a moment it seems as if they are both about to reject Marlow as a suitable husband for Kate; however, Kate wisely makes a condition: that if Hardcastle finds Marlow 'less impudent' and she finds him 'more presuming', then they will review the situation.

Tony Lumpkin retrieves Constance's jewels from Mrs Hardcastle and gives them to Hastings. Almost immediately Constance begs her aunt to let her have the jewels, but Mrs Hardcastle fobs her off with remarks about the unsuitability of ornamenting the young. In an aside Mrs Hardcastle tells Tony that she is trying to hang on to the jewels in order to pass them on to him. 'Tell her they're lost' says Lumpkin, offering to be a witness to this fact. Mrs Hardcastle does so, and the ensuing conversation, in the light of the crisis that is to follow, is quietly ironic as Mrs Hardcastle advises Constance to learn resignation. She promises to lend the girl her own unfashionable semi-precious garnets, and goes out to fetch them. Moments later a calamitous wailing breaks out as Mrs Hardcastle discovers her desk has been rifled and the jewels are missing. The irony of the previous lines rouses the audience to hilarity as Lumpkin reiterates that he will bear witness to the fact that the jewels are missing. Mrs Hardcastle bemoans the fact that her son is unable to distinguish between 'jest and earnest', yet another irony as it is she, amongst others, who is taken in by the boy's tricks.

One of the principal sections of the play is then enacted: it consists of Kate's attempts to discover the real person who hides behind the serious earnestness of Marlow. He mistakes her for a maid, as she wears her plain dress for the evening. Imagining her to be one of the lower classes he pays her pretty compliments, such as he was quite unable to pay Kate in their earlier encounter. Kate manages to steer the conversation round to this meeting, mentioning Marlow's seeming timidity in her presence. Marlow dismisses the Kate whom he met earlier as a 'mere, awkward, squinting thing', and speaks of his gallantry at the Ladies Club in London where he, together with a number of the members whom he mentions by name, 'keep up the spirit of the place'. Kate refers to the quilts in the bedrooms that she has embroidered: on an impulse Marlow seizes her hand and tries to take her upstairs in order to examine her handiwork. As she is struggling to free herself Hardcastle enters, outraged at Marlow's encroachment into his household and now surprised to see this behaviour towards his daughter, especially as earlier she had described his manner as timid. Kate makes another condition – she wants a brief time in which to demonstrate that Marlow has only 'the faults that will pass off with time, and the virtues that will improve with age'. Much against his better judgement Hardcastle agrees.

Commentary

The central feature of this scene is the dichotomy that Hardcastle and Kate find themselves in over their conflicting views of Marlow's character. Is he impudent and overweening or is he timidly modest and open to too much feeling? That neither of these views describes his basic disposition leads us to suppose that this is yet another case of mistaken identity. In striking a bargain with her father that she will discover more of Marlow's character, Kate leaves the audience to assume that she has a plan in mind and that this will help to advance the plot in the next act.

Disguise and deceit, two related practices, play a part in this act. Kate may be said to be in some kind of a disguise, although she merely wears the plain dress she habitually assumes in the evenings. It is enough, together with her importuning – a form of deceit – to trick Marlow into believing that she is a barmaid. His encounter with Kate is strongly contrasted with their earlier meeting in Act 2, and through it Kate now gains an added dimension on Marlow's behaviour. This meeting, however, serves to reinforce Hardcastle's unfavourable impression of the young man.

Deceit reveals Mrs Hardcastle in a new light to the audience. To this point in the play she has been presented as a faithful wife and doting mother, although hankering after a more sociable life than her country environment will allow. In his presentation of her, Goldsmith enlists the sympathy of the audience. Suddenly the audience has to revise its opinions of a character: Mrs Hardcastle is seen as a dishonest woman, intent on misappropriating her niece's jewels in order to give them to her son. Justice quickly catches up with her in the farcical situation which ensues by the engineering of Lumpkin. The audience warms to him as he rights this wrong and at the same time plans to send Constance off with her rightful dowry.

Act 4

Summary

A letter arrives for Hardcastle telling him that Marlow's father, Sir Charles Marlow, will be arriving shortly. Constance apprises Hastings of this information. He tells her that they must be on their way before the arrival of Sir Charles, as he is known to him, and possibly the elopement plan would be discovered. Lumpkin has promised fresh horses for the journey. Constance enquires after her jewels and Hastings explains that he has given them to Marlow to guard.

As Constance and Hastings leave the stage Marlow enters, musing on the strangeness of Hastings' behaviour in sending him the box of jewellery to look after. The only place he had for its deposition was in the post-coach standing outside the house, so he has passed it on to the 'landlady' for safekeeping. When Hastings returns Marlow's mind is still much set on the 'barmaid' he encountered earlier. Interrupting his reverie, Hastings is horrified to learn that Mrs Hardcastle is looking after Constance's casket of jewels, but he quickly hides his unease and determines that, if needs must, he will leave without the fortune.

Hardcastle enters and complains to Marlow that his servants have been getting drunk and disorderly. Again the mistaken identity leads to a humorous situation. Marlow protests that he has told the servants to drink plenty in order to line the 'innkeeper's' coffers, and Jeremy, one of the retinue by this time incapacitated, corroborates the report: Hardcastle, naturally, is outraged at the familiarity of Marlow and his company and with sarcasm he offers him various pieces of furniture and decoration. Marlow's shouts for his bill are interrupted by Hardcastle's incensed complaint that Sir Charles has led him to expect a person of breeding, instead of which he has met with a coxcomb and a bully. As the indignant man sweeps out of the room the truth strikes Marlow – he has mistaken the house. Distraught, he tries to get information from Kate who hurries in. She claims (another deception on her part) that she is a poor relation appointed to act as a housekeeper; and she assures Marlow that he is in Mr Hardcastle's house. Chagrined, he confesses that he mistook Kate for the barmaid. She pretends to weep at the notion she has done anything to disoblige Marlow, who is deeply touched at this mark of tenderness, nevertheless, because he imagines that Kate and he are of a different social standing, he finds an 'honourable connexion' impossible. When he leaves her, Kate determines that she will continue to pretend to be the poor relation, but nevertheless let her father know about the deceptions Marlow has suffered. Tony has arrived with fresh horses – although the jewels are still with Mrs Hardcastle. On cue Lumpkin's mother comes in speaking of the jewels which she intends to guard until Tony and Constance are safely married; then she will hand the fortune over to the pair. For Mrs Hardcastle's benefit the young couple dally together with a pretence of fondness. They are interrupted by the entrance of Diggory with a letter for Lumpkin. As the boy is barely literate he has difficulty in making out the contents. Constance recognises the handwriting as that of Hastings, so she gains the letter from him, pretending to read a message about a cock fight. As she attempts to thrust the letter away, Lumpkin snatches it and asks Mrs Hardcastle to read it to him. She does so: Hastings is waiting at the end of the garden for Constance; the post coach is ready, but fresh horses are needed; speed is needed or Mrs Hardcastle (referred to as 'the hag') will suspect a plot. In an expostulation of rage Mrs Hardcastle determines to use the horses to take Constance to her Aunt Pedigree, who, she is sure, will keep the girl secure. Lumpkin is to travel on his own horse to look after the party.

Constance rounds on Lumpkin, bemoaning his stupidity. Hastings enters and accuses Lumpkin of betraying himself and Constance. Marlow has realised that Lumpkin was the instigator of the plot to deceive him and on his entry he accuses Tony of being an idiot. Accusations fly and mount up, stopped short by a servant instructing Constance that all is ready for the journey: she must hurry for they are to travel thirty miles before the next morning. The quarrel switches to Hastings and Marlow, for the latter is still smarting over the deceptions practised on him. Constance draws their attention by urging Hastings to be constant to her for three years until she comes of age. She leaves to begin the journey.

During this time Tony Lumpkin has been in a reverie. Suddenly he announces he has a plan to save the situation. Hastings and Marlow are to meet him in two hours' time at the end of the garden.

Commentary

In this act several people become aware of the deceptions practised on them: Marlow learns that the house he has been staying in is not an inn but the house of his future father-in-law; Mrs Hardcastle realises that Hastings is about to elope with Constance and that any hint of matchmaking between Constance and Tony Lumpkin was an illusion. Thus the complications of the plot begin to be unravelled. A minor complication occurs, too: Kate still deceives Marlow, but she changes her role from that of a barmaid to a poor relation. Although other people gradually realise the truth, Marlow is the last to come to terms with Kate's real nature and station.

The letter which Mrs Hardcastle intercepts is a stock device within the Georgian theatre; but Goldsmith simplifies the use. Generally the letter misleads the recipient in sowing seeds of doubt or misinformation; Goldsmith, through the letter, presents Mrs Hardcastle with the truth about the planned elopement and with Hastings' true opinion of her. This revelation is made the harder for Dorothy Hardcastle as a matter of an hour or so previous he was flattering her.

As in the previous act instances of irony abound: it is there in Marlow's innocent action of passing the jewels to Mrs Hardcastle to guard: it is present, too, verbally in the exchange of Hardcastle and Marlow, and in Kate's talk of rank in society with Marlow. But as the truth behind each deception is revealed the opportunities for the playwright to make ironic comment on the situation diminish. Lest, however, members of the audience should imagine that the impetus of the plot has run down before the final act is reached, interest is given a fresh boost by Tony Lumpkin's final speech in which he hints that he has a plan for retrieving the seemingly lost happiness of Hastings and

Constance. It is at this point that the subplot assumes a temporary prominence in order to drive the play towards its resolution.

Act 5, Scene 1

Summary

The indication of the servant that Mrs Hardcastle's coach will have travelled thirty miles and that Sir Charles Marlow has arrived, informs the audience that a period of time has passed since the ending of Act 4. Hastings repairs to the end of the garden as Tony Lumpkin re-enters.

Hardcastle enters with Sir Charles: the audience is left in some doubt as to the way in which Hardcastle has learnt of Marlow's misassumption, but he and his companion are heartily amused by it. They go on to discuss the liaison of the two families which will be brought about by the possible marriage of Kate and Marlow if they find that they love each other. Marlow enters, still apologising for his conduct: conversation quickly turns to Kate, and Marlow speaks of his respect for her and of Kate's reserve in her approach to him. Sir Charles and Hardcastle assume that a courtship has taken place and that it only remains for the marriage to be celebrated. Marlow's parting shot is to assure the two fathers, in a neat example of antithesis, that he 'saw the lady without emotion, and parted without reluctance'. When Kate enters the room she is quizzed by the gentlemen on whether Marlow showed any expressions of tenderness towards her. She assures them that he spoke much of love and a permanent attachment. Sir Charles is certain that his son would not employ a 'forward canting ranting manner' and so doubts the truth of Kate's words. However, Kate has a plan: in half an hour's time Sir Charles and her father are to hide behind a screen in the room and they will hear Marlow make a declaration of his passion for her.

Commentary

The final act is divided into three short scenes, and these help to give a feeling of increasing pace as the play proceeds towards its final resolution. This is a characteristic device of plays written for the Georgian stage. A further theatrical device is that of delaying the entry of one of the characters until the last act of the play: this causes some conjecture on the nature of the character who will finally appear, as well as adding interest once he becomes evident. A third device is hinted at in Kate's plan to secrete the two elderly gentlemen behind the screen: again, several playwrights of the period use a screen in order to bring the action to its fulfilment. Four years after the production of *She Stoops to Conquer* Richard Brinsley Sheridan (1751–1816) was to use a screen scene in *The School for Scandal*, a memorable development of Goldsmith's management of the device.

Act 5, Scene 2

Summary

The scene changes to the *Back of the Garden* where the audience sees Hastings waiting for Tony Lumpkin to put his plan into operation. Lumpkin enters dressed in his riding gear, spattered with mud as he has ridden for a couple of hours accompanying Mrs Hardcastle and Constance in the coach. Hastings learns that Lumpkin has guided the coach on a circular route. Instead of taking the occupants to Aunt Pedigree's house he has brought them home again, finally leaving the coach stuck in the horse pond at the bottom of the garden.

Mrs Hardcastle enters in an almost deranged state, made the worse by Lumpkin pretending that they are on Crackskull Common, a haunt of thieves. In her terror she mistakes Hardcastle for a highwayman and, at Tony's suggestion, hides in a bush. Lumpkin pretends to Hardcastle that his mother and Constance are safely with Aunt Pedigree. He is anxious to get his father back into the house so that he may help Hastings and Constance in their elopement, but Mrs Hardcastle, by this time fearing that the 'highwayman' will be about to murder her son, runs out from the bush and offers money and watches in exchange for safety. Gently Hardcastle reassures his wife that she is within forty yards of her own house. Both of them round on Tony Lumpkin, realising that he has performed another of his tricks, and Hardcastle takes his wife indoors.

Finally Hastings and Constance enter. Constance has made up her mind that an elopement is not the answer; she is prudent enough to realise that flight without the fortune would be unwise. She resolves instead to go to Hardcastle and ask for 'compassion and justice'. Reluctantly Hastings concurs with Constance.

Commentary

This scene is unique in as much as the discomfiture of a character is made uproariously funny. In retaliation for her treatment of Constance

Mrs Hardcastle herself suffers 'the mistakes of a night' – a seemingly dangerous journey, the horsepond, Crackskull Common and a highwayman.

In commenting on Act 1 Scene 2 mention was made of the fictional countryside which Stingo the landlord and Tony Lumpkin created. In this scene it is again in evidence, in the frightening Crackskull Common, the haunt of highwaymen. Presumably the description Lumpkin gives to Hastings slightly earlier in the scene of the journey down Featherbed-lane and over Heavy-Tree Heath is a factual account of the area surrounding Hardcastle's house.

Act 5, Scene 3

Summary
Kate tells Sir Charles that she has a plan whereby he will hear Marlow make a declaration of his love to her. Sir Charles goes to fetch Hardcastle, his fellow-partaker in the plot; soon afterwards the pair re-enter and hide behind a screen in order to eavesdrop on Kate and Marlow.

Marlow tells Kate he has come to say farewell to her. At first Kate tries to persuade Marlow to remain for a few days longer. However Marlow seems to be determined to leave, although the factor that had prompted him to go now seems less pressing. Kate speaks, slightly bitterly, of the difference in her fortunes and that of 'her's you came down to visit'. Immediately Marlow responds, and speaks of his admiration for Kate; so enthusiastic does he become that he decides to remain in order to introduce Kate to his father; kneeling before her he speaks of his growing delight in her presence.

It is at this point that Sir Charles and Hardcastle obtrude on the scene: sarcastically they enquire whether his present position reflects his 'cold contempt' for Kate. Marlow immediately discovers that Kate is not the maid, but his host's daughter. She laughs at his discomforture, asking him which of his two personages should be addressed, – the shy young gentleman or the rake about town? Together they retire to the back of the stage as Mrs Hardcastle and her son enter. Mrs Hardcastle presumes that Constance and Hastings have, by this time, left for London. On hearing the name Hastings, Sir Charles speaks of the worth of the young man and his suitability as a husband. Mrs Hardcastle's thoughts immediately turn to the fortune which is still safe with her. Hardcastle reminds his wife that if Tony Lumpkin has not agreed to marry Constance by the time he is twenty-one then the jewels revert to her.

All are surprised to see Hastings and Constance Neville enter the room. Hastings explains that they have returned in order to appeal to Hardcastle's humanity and to secure from his tenderness, rather than his justice, the fortune. Mrs Hardcastle tries to dismiss the speeches of Constance and Hastings as the whimpering conclusion of a sentimental novel. Hardcastle has the last ploy in the play to draw on. He asks Lumpkin if he refuses to marry Constance. Tony reminds him he can't refuse until he is of age. It is then that Hardcastle breaks the news to him that he is already of age; Mrs Hardcastle has kept Lumpkin's true age from him. Immediately the boy refuses Constance Neville as his 'true and lawful wife'. Marlow wishes his friend and his future wife much happiness and then Hardcastle completes the scene by joining the hands of Kate and Marlow together producing a stage picture of the couples' future life together. He declares that the 'Mistakes of the Night' will be followed by the merry-making of the morning.

Commentary

The last scene of a play is, of course, one in which remaining mysteries are disclosed and a hint of the future is given. In this scene Sir Charles and Hardcastle discover that Marlow can make his proposal without bashfulness but with propriety: Marlow discovers who Kate is; and Lumpkin discovers that he has come of age. Tony announces his independence of a betrothal to Constance; whilst the marriages of Hastings with Constance and Marlow with Kate are anticipated. The plot depended on Marlow mistaking the house of his future father-in-law as an inn. He learnt of his mistake in that field in Act 4. However an extension of that was his misidentification of Kate as a barmaid, and, in order to maintain interest in the plot, it is not until the final scene of the play that Marlow discovers that she is the person he originally set out to meet. Thus in the growing relationship of Marlow and Kate in this scene Goldsmith uses cleverly the device of parallels – to Kate Marlow has two natures; and Marlow suddenly perceives that he has known Kate under two natures. In the revealed knowledge of each other they discover the unity lying behind the appearance of duality.

Epilogue

The epilogue usually consisted of a light-hearted rhymed comment on the play, light-hearted even when the play was a tragedy. It was a transition point in drawing the audience back to the everyday world; in some way the epilogue usually expressed a plea for the audience to show its approval of the piece. Epilogues were spoken either before a specially painted drop curtain (or *rideau*) or in front of the heavy green proscenium curtain which fell at the end of the play.

Mrs Bulkley, who played the part of Kate Hardcastle, speaks the epilogue in the person of a barmaid. She begins and ends with the wish to obtain the audience's appreciation for the piece. Principally she considers the five stages of the barmaid's life; these, of course, parallel the five acts of the play. The first stage shows the nervous country girl who has just been hired to work at the inn; the second stage shows a highly competent barmaid; the third stage reveals her as the mistress of a chop house in the City; the fourth stage shows her married to the squire, playing at cards (spadille is the ace of spades) half the night: the final stage is left to the imagination of the audience. This structure for the epilogue is suggested by Jacques' lines in *As You Like It*, one of which is quoted: 'We have our exits and our entrances'. Jacques then goes on to speak of the 'seven ages of man', the stages in man's life from infancy to senility. The eighteenth-century painter William Hogarth (1697–1764) made several series of paintings based on the stages in the life of a rake (a worthless spendthrift) and the stages in an unsuccessful marriage. Goldsmith would have seen engravings of these, as they were highly popular, and such series also may have suggested the form of the epilogue to him.

Three other epilogues, written prior to this, had been found unacceptable by the speakers and by the manager of Covent Garden.

4 THEMES AND ISSUES

4.1 AN OVERVIEW OF THE CHAPTER

She Stoops to Conquer is more than an example of narration by means
of actors, although this element is present. An extra dimension is given
to the plot by the development of several related themes: the plot hangs
principally on Tony Lumpkin's deceit in suggesting to Marlow and
Hastings that his stepfather's house is an inn and the ensuing problems
caused by this mistaken identification. Further complications arise
from Kate's decision to allow Marlow to imagine that when she is in her
homely attire she is a barmaid: thus to some extent the theme of disguise runs through the play also, and this is touched upon at several
points in the narrative. In the gradual resolution of the plot it is important that errors of identity are cleared away so that the participants
in the comedy may recognise the true character of their fellows. In turn
this leads to a philosophical idea: in the discovery of the truth about
identity, an element of self-discovery may be present. Thus it is that
Marlow's divided nature (his brashness of approach on the one hand
and his unnatural reserve on the other) is brought ultimately to a
harmonious unity, and he discovers how to cope with the opposite sex.

Inevitably any playwright of worth gives an insight into the period
about which he is writing and Goldsmith is no exception. We learn of
various attitudes about country life and of the views of people on urban
living. In this there is some kind of dichotomy, for the town, and more
especially London, signifies a sophisticated and fashionable way of life,
whilst time in the country moves at a different pace and different values

pertain. So it is that Goldsmith surpasses mere historical comment and invests the two contrasting ways of living with differing symbolic clusters. Other ideas, at first little more than background information, assume an importance as the play proceeds. In *She Stoops to Conquer*, for example, the saying 'An Englishman's home is his castle' is viewed in terms of Marlow's and Hardcastle's attitude towards the house on the hill. As an audience watches the play it learns, too, a certain amount about eighteenth-century habits of travel, in both Hastings' and Marlow's journey as well as that ill-fated ride that Mrs Hardcastle and her niece take, and the interlinked conventions about taverns, inns and other places in which travellers lodged overnight. There are further reflections of eighteenth-century social life with which we shall deal later in this chapter.

So much for the content of the play. But we need to go further and discover the generic roots of Goldsmith's idea of comedy. This is important, for these, too, are an element in 'what the play is about'. We have to relate *She Stoops to Conquer* to the other plays of its time, for none is an isolated phenomenon, and we must consider the playwright's own responses to these plays. Because this is the foundational principle on which Goldsmith wrote it seems best to consider this point first, and from there to study the literary content and Goldsmith's use of his contemporary (and to us, historical) background.

4.2 THE GEORGIAN REPERTOIRE

In 1773, the year in which *She Stoops to Conquer* was first performed, the London stage presented spectators with a variety of dramatic entertainments. Certain plays of William Shakespeare (1564–1616), often altered in order to accommodate the tastes of the day, were presented; David Garrick, for example, had shortened *The Taming of the Shrew* and presented it as an afterpiece (a minor entertainment following the principal play) entitled *Catharine and Petrouchio*; Nahum Tate (1652–1715) playwright and hymn writer had radically altered *King Lear*, giving the play a jubilant ending for the virtuous. A few of the Restoration comedies were given occasional performances, although the situations described in them were often found offensive. The writing of tragedy was popular, and in Goldsmith's essay 'The Chinese goes to see a play' it is thought that Lien Chi Altangi is watching

Douglas, one of the most popular of tragedies written by a Church of Scotland minister, John Home (1722–1808). A wide range of operettas and farces was also produced, often as a makeweight for the final part of the evening's programme.

One very popular type of comedy was known as the 'comedy of manners'. In this the characters tended to be middle-class townspeople. Playwrights used the characters to demonstrate the extremes of social behaviour, and the absurdity that an excessive regard for social convention and formalised politeness creates. The range of such characters would include fops, back-bites, scheming wives, lecherous young men, and the occasional old one: indeed, writers present us with a series of caricatures of the people of the town. Not only their behaviour is artificial; so is their speech, as sparkling epigrams are tossed from one speaker to another. This world is a far cry from the rural retreat of the Hardcastles and the plain words which are heard therein. To some degree audiences were surprised by the contrast.

4.3 SENTIMENTAL COMEDY

The nature of Sentimental Comedy

One development of the comedy of manners led to that category of comedy known as the 'sentimental drama'. In this the characters were essentially ordinary people. Their prevailing characteristic was that they were highly virtuous for the most part, wishing to expend acts of kindness on others. In this they certainly put into practice the aphorism of Archbishop John Tillotson (1630–94) on benevolence: 'There is no sensual Pleasure in the World comparable to the Delight and Satisfaction that a good Man takes in doing good.'

Almost always some kind of moral element exists in the play, either in the form of a problem, or as the need for some sort of moral pursuit. Obviously, in order to confront the audience with this problem several of the characters present a lack of virtue in their lives, if only temporarily: for example a repeated problem in sentimental dramas is that a character keeps a mistress who, under moral pressure, he feels he must relinquish. The sheer goodness of the virtuous converts those whose lives are lacking in it, and repentance is expressed in lengthy, moralistic speeches. Sentimental drama is often guilty of exaggeration: the fundamental moral goodness of human nature is stressed to an inordinate degree, for this is man as he ought to be, rather than as he is; any acts unworthy of his nature are rapidly followed by remorse and rectification; reformation constantly leads to general happiness. Thus, it can be seen that sentimental drama is one that preaches and moralistically instructs. John Hawksworth (1715-75), writing of the comedies of Richard Cumberland, (1732-1811) which are typical of this genre, spells out the playwright's earnest intention:

> [he] has interested the passions in the cause of virtue, and endeavoured to correct the vices and follies of a dissolute age, at the very moment when he is administering to its pleasures. . .

As with the action, the language of sentimental drama was exaggeratedly moralistic. It tended to be somewhat formalised too. However, as a compensation, witty turns of phrase were often employed, which helped a little to decongest the cloying situations. Nevertheless, the language was often inappropriate to the character speaking, for the playwright often used each as his own mouthpiece. This point William Whiteland took up in his prologue to *The Roman Father*, praising the discipline of the play's author in expunging unsuitable diction:

> Nay, even each moral *sentimental* stroke,
> Where not the character, but the poet spoke,
> He lopp'd as foreign to his chaste design;
> Nor spared a useless, though a golden, line.

Obviously, in this use of language, there is a link with the comedy of manners. The stress on benevolence, pity and repentance effectively curbed humour in both the situations of the comedy and in the language, for this tended to work against an affective response. These comedies 'homilies in dialogue' the essayist Richard Steele (1672-1729), called them, were a method of moral teaching; amusement, laughter or bawdry were entirely out of place in them.

Furthermore, sentimental dramatists intensified the moral impact on the audience by removing all that was superfluous to the main thread of the plot. Thus the subplot was eliminated from comedy, and with it went the range of amusing low life characters who provided a foil to the principal roles. The emotional drive which the sentimental dramatist employed was responsible not only for the tone of the play but also for an ironing out of the class structure of the participants.

An Example of Sentimental Comedy: *The West Indian*

Two years before *She Stoops to Conquer* was published Richard Cumberland wrote a comedy which may serve as an archetype of the sentimental drama: this was *The West Indian*. The complicated plot revolves around Belcour, a young man brought up in Jamaica who has recently arrived in London. He is presumed to be a foundling but is in fact the grandson of a wealthy dealer. Belcour is generous to a fault to those who attempt to make a claim on him, and it is this excess of generosity, together with Belcour's innocence in society, which prompts a series of situations through which he passes with virtue unscathed, but luckily with the ability also to advance in wisdom. His largess is rewarded at the end of the play when he is discovered to be the heir to his grandfather's fortune – in such plays 'relationship, like murder', will out as Mr Puff says in the burlesque *The Critic* by Richard Brinsley Sheridan (1751–1816) of this situation.

So much for the outline of *The West Indian*. When we look at the language of this play and the sentiments expressed, we see that it is a far cry from the unaffected language of Goldsmith's play. Two examples will be sufficient to make this clear. It is important for actors in a sentimental play to elicit pity from the audience, and this is achieved through speeches in which the pathos of a person's situation is exploited. Near the beginning of the play Belcour recounts to his unknown father, Stockwell, the perils of his supposed orphan state:

> . . . I am the offspring of distress, and every child of sorrow is my brother; while I have hands to hold, therefore, I will hold them open to mankind; but, sir, my passions are my masters; they take me where they will; and, oftentimes, they leave to reason and to virtue nothing but my wishes and my sighs.

In addition to this pathos there is also in the situation a strong element of irony. The last moments of the play are spent in Stockwell revealing to Belcour that they are father and son. Again, emotional play is made of the information, and sententiousness colours each of Belcour's exclamations:

STOCKWELL: I am your father.

BELCOUR: My father! – Do I live?

STOCKWELL: I am your father.

BELCOUR: It is too much – my happiness overpowers me – to gain a friend, and find a father, is too much: I blush to think how little I deserve you.

The moralistic tone is carried through to Belcour's final speech:

> . . . whenever you perceive me deviating into error or offence, bring only to my mind the providence of this night, and I will turn to reason and obey.

An audience in the theatre today would find Belcour's overt stress on his own virtue embarrassing. Not so in the latter part of the eighteenth century: audiences found such characters appealing and evocative of admiration. However, the drawing of Goldsmith's characters in *She Stoops to Conquer* is a far cry from Cumberland's Belcour and it is possible to appreciate the extent to which the sentimental tone was missed, and the way in which the comedy was on occasion misconstrued to be a farce.

In his poem *The Retaliation* Goldsmith briefly gave his view of the impediment in Cumberland's vision of comedy. He was

> A flattering painter, who made it his care
> To draw men as they ought to be, not as they are.
> His gallants are all faultless, his women divine,
> And comedy wonders at being so fine . . .

Low-life scenes deprived *She Stoops to Conquer* of the finesse of which Goldsmith speaks in the poem; and compared with Belcour, Goldsmith's hero Marlow is a very unheroic character.

4.4 DISAFFECTION FOR SENTIMENTAL COMEDY

General

But we must not imagine that the sentimental drama was universally applauded; there were writers who realised the limitations that it imposed. In France it was referred to as the 'Comedie Larmoyant' or 'Weeping Comedy', and the philosopher Voltaire (1694–1778), called the genre the 'Tradesman's Tragedy', an excellent description which summed up both the social level of the content and the morose tone. In England one of the activists against sentiment was Samuel Foote (1720–77), the manager of the Little Theatre in the Haymarket. He devised a puppet play entitled *The Handsome Housemaid or Piety in Pattens* in which he ridiculed genteel comedy. When the reviews of *She Stoops to Conquer* came to be written, the critic of the *Morning Chronicle* claimed that Foote's production was a helpful preparation for the subsequent happy reception of Goldsmith's play. Even Richard Cumberland, the doyen of sentimentalists, could distance himself from the subject. The speaker of the epilogue to his play *The Impostor* threatened:

I come to laugh, or I come here no more.

Goldsmith and Sentimental Drama

The Westminster Magazine for January 1773 carried an article by Goldsmith entitled 'An Essay on the Theatre or a Comparison between Laughing and Sentimental Comedy'. It has sometimes been claimed that this was written to prepare theatregoers for the play that was to be staged in March, although it is open to question how effective a form of preparation this would be. The writing is, however, a statement of Goldsmith's belief in the value of a kind of comedy which makes people laugh rather than serving a moral and didactic purpose. Goldsmith pointed out that traditionally the objectives of comedy and tragedy differed; comedy, as defined by the ancient Greek philosopher Aristotle (384–322 BC), was designed to represent 'the Frailties of the Lower part of Mankind', whilst tragedy was 'an Exhibition of the Misfortune of the Great'. It follows that comedy must centre on low and middle life and so ridiculously present the characters and their follies that laughter ensues. Instead, Goldsmith claims, the stage has been taken over by sentimental drama, with its different way of looking at the characters:

If they happen to have Faults or Foibles, the Spectator is taught not only to pardon, but to applaud them, in consideration of the good-ness of their hearts; so that Folly, instead of being ridiculed, is commended, and the Comedy aims at touching our Passions without the power of being truly pathetic.

He goes on to compare the sentimental drama with the sentimental novel. In this the scenes and characters are stock types and remarkably similar to those found in the parallel dramas:

> It is only sufficient to raise the Character a little, to deck out the Hero with a Ribband, or give the Heroine a Title, then to put an Insipid Dialogue without Character or Humour, into their mouths, give them mighty good hearts, very fine cloaths, furnish a new sett of Scenes, make a Pathetic Scene or two, with a sprinkling of tender melancholy Conversation through the whole, and there is no doubt but all the Ladies will cry, and all the Gentlemen applaud.

Throughout the essay Goldsmith reiterates that the sentimental comedy is an unwholesome mix of tragedy and comedy with the result that a 'species of Bastard Tragedy' emerges. The art of comedy needs to be recovered, that once again humour can find its place on the stage and laughter in the auditorium.

No more for true comedy was given in the essay: that was to come two months later in the production of *She Stoops to Conquer*. In the light of Goldsmith's essay we can see the revolt against the sentimental drama in this: there are the scenes of low life as well as those of the middle class; Marlow is no bedecked hero exuding benevolence; Kate has nothing of the insipidity of a sentimental heroine; Mrs Hardcastle is made a figure of fun and left stuck in a horsepond; the dialogue appears to be naturalistic rather than one peppered with witty aphorisms; the location is an unfashionable area of the countryside, rather than the centre of social interaction.

The critic of the *Morning Chronicle* recognised Goldsmith's break with the moribund convention of the sentimental drama:

> he has offered the public a true comic picture, and altho' it differed most essentially in manner, stile and finishing from those which have of late years been received . . . laughter sat on every face, mirth and extatic [sic] joy, the proper effects of comedy, universally prevailed, and the most impartial, and repeated plaudits were showered down on the author.

Dr Johnson, who was a member of the first night audience, concurred with the critic's opinion: 'I know of no comedy for many years that has so much exhilarated an audience, that has answered so much the great end of comedy – making an audience merry.' Oliver Goldsmith had launched a successful attack on what the *London Magazine* referred to as 'that monster Sentimental Comedy'.

4.5 LITERARY DEVICES IN THE PLAY

Deception and Disguise

Let us turn from the intention underpinning the play and look at the content. The device which remains firmly in one's mind after seeing the play performed is that instigated by Tony Lumpkin in tricking Hastings and Marlow into believing that Hardcastle's house is an inn. The humour mainly hangs on this mistaken identity. In this connection we recall the subtitle of the piece: *The Mistakes of a Night*. It is true, then, that much of the comedy is concerned with deception and the resultant errors in identifying places and people; but reflection shows us that this farcical joke perpetrated by Tony Lumpkin is multiplied in other ways. Kate and Hastings prolong Lumpkin's deception and keep Marlow in the belief that he is sojourning at an inn. Kate compounds the deception by pretending to be the barmaid at this hostelry. Here an element akin to the related devices of deception and misidentification is also at work: this is the dramatic convention of disguise. It is a convention in as much as characters are taken in by disguise with a gullibility that only holds good within the framework of the play. Lesser deceptions decorate these major ones: Mrs Hardcastle has kept Tony in ignorance of his real age; Constance Neville has kept the seriousness of her romance with Hastings from her aunt; the business of Constance's jewellery weaves a web of deception in which Constance, Mrs Hardcastle, Tony and, unwittingly, Marlow are all involved; Tony Lumpkin acts out an elaborate deception in taking his aunt for a circular ride – the converse of the short-cut to the inn on which he directed the two travellers at the beginning of the play; and Hardcastle and his friend Sir Charles deceive Marlow about the privacy of his interview with Kate by becoming voyeurs. There may possibly be other verbal deceptions perpetrated – about these Goldsmith gives us only a few clues: we can deduce from his inaccuracy in the telling of them, that Hardcastle's anecdotes about his military campaigns may be fictions: we can only guess which of the countryside surrounding the house in Tony Lumpkin's descriptions is 'real' and which is the figment of his imagination.

How does Goldsmith make dramatic use of this device of disguise and mistaken identity? First, he uses it in order to establish and advance the plot. The plot hangs on the deception set up in the first act by Lumpkin that Hardcastle's house is an inn. It is advanced as soon as Hastings, Constance and Kate discover the deception and make use of it to further their own purposes; and it becomes elaborated by Kate's pretence that she is a barmaid. Thus the plot gains in momentum, and each time a fresh deception is practised the interest of the audience is recharged. The sub-plot (a return to an older practice) is so carefully interwoven with the main plot that some would query whether it is identifiable as a separate entity: if we allow it to be so, then this consists of Hastings' elopement with Constance, in itself a form of deception, and the numerous lies which are told in gaining and retrieving Constance's fortune. This does not become a separate issue until Act 2 and the situation is a further example of new material used to gain added interest. The sub-plot continues until Act 5 when, in the journey made by Mrs Hardcastle and Constance we see a parallel of the night ride that might have been made had the two lovers eloped.

Secondly, Goldsmith uses the device of disguise and mistaken identity as the basis for dramatic irony. In this the audience is aware of layers of relevance in situations and in the dialogue of which some, or all, of the characters on stage remain in ignorance. The first meeting of Marlow and Hastings with Tony Lumpkin sparks off ironical remarks. Lumpkin paints a picture of the Hardcastle family as seen through his own eyes; the two travellers have only come across descriptions of the family by report, but the audience has had an opportunity to assimilate the characteristics of its respective members.

On the travellers' arrival at the 'inn' they keep the audience amused by recounting the fate of 'rumbling mansions' in their conversion to hostelries. In order to give both variety and complexity to this device other characters become aware of the mistake, but Marlow is in ignorance of the truth until the end of Act 4. At this point he recapitulates on the dramatic interest his situation has held for the audience: 'I have been ... rendered contemptible, driven into ill-manners, despised, insulted, laughed at.'

Irony runs through the section of Act 3 in which Marlow mistakes Kate for the barmaid and there is an opportunity for him to convey to this *altera persona* some of his opinions about Kate. Although Kate and the audience know the true situation there is a danger at one stage that Marlow may see through the deception: 'I don't quite like this chit. She looks knowing methinks.' This introduces momentarily an element of suspense into a romantically humorous scene.

On Mrs Hardcastle's insistence Constance and Lumpkin are forced to pretend that they are in love, if only to allay any suspicions that an elopement is in the planning. Thus, in their dalliance, there are implications of which Mrs Hardcastle is unaware:

> I'm sure I've always lov'd cousin Con's hazel eyes, and her pretty long fingers, that she twists this way and that, over the haspicholls, like a parcel of bobbins.

What exactly the two performers on stage do during these interchanges in order to reinforce the irony is a matter for interesting conjecture. This is obviously a broader, more humorous use of irony than the earlier mentioned incidents. At their first meeting, to allay Mrs Hardcastle's fears Hastings ingratiates himself with her by means of gross flattery, a further form of deception and, because Mrs Hardcastle is not fashionable, of irony. By means of this conversation Goldsmith is able to satirise notions of fashionable London society, as well as indulging in ironic comment.

A playwright may make an ironic comment through situation as well as by means of dialogue. In Mrs Hardcastle's encounter with the 'highwayman' – in fact, her own husband – Goldsmith seems to be making a comment on her inability to recognise the truth about people, whether it be in her idolisation of Tony Lumpkin, the flattery of Hastings, or her own powers of self-deception in believing she is a youthfully fashionable socialite. In studying the play students are advised to look for other instances of this slightly less obvious form of ironical comment, especially in relation to the character of people.

A use that Goldsmith makes of the convention of disguise and unmasking is to suggest that characters in the play discover their true identities. This idea is taken up several times, although it is most strongly expressed in the discovery which Marlow makes as the play progresses. In Act 2 he expresses the fear that, in his approach to members of the opposite sex, lies a divided character: with 'females of another class' such as barmaids, courtesans, and prostitutes, Marlow is 'impudent enough', but with 'women of reputation', society people, he is 'such an idiot, such a trembler'. Goldsmith shows us these two approaches in action, with Kate and with the 'barmaid', in itself an ironic situation. By Act 5 Marlow can make a bold, patterned address to Kate which stays within the bounds of propriety:

> every moment that I converse with you, steals in some new grace, heightens the picture, and gives it stronger expression. What at first seem'd rustic plainness, now appears refin'd simplicity. What seem'd forward assurance, now strikes me as the result of courageous innocence and conscious virtue.

Thus Marlow discovers a balanced attitude towards Kate. He doesn't achieve this by his own efforts, but with her help, patience and wisdom. She is the facilitator of his discovery.

In the same vein Tony Lumpkin discovers that he is not simply a booby and a wastrel prankster. The first half of the play may seem to establish that character, but in the second half we see Lumpkin governing his powers of invention and using them positively to help Constance gain her fortune, to aid both her and Hastings in their elopement, although unsuccessfully through no fault of his own, and then to bring Constance safely back to the Hardcastle home so that she may be reunited with Hastings. This time the discovery of innate goodness has been without the tutelage of another person.

Freedom and 'Liberty-hall'

A further idea that is explored in *She Stoops to Conquer* is that of liberty. Hardcastle sets the tone for this in his welcome to his visitors: 'This is Liberty-hall'. To a liberal landowner such as Hardcastle the remark seems perfectly apposite; but to several people living in the home it might seem an ironical claim, especially to Tony Lumpkin and Constance Neville. Constance has all the characteristics of a poor relation – with the exception that she will in three years' time receive a fortune. The death of her father has forced her to reside with her aunt, a person who is difficult to live with and who, in her speech to Constance in Act 4 on discovering the elopement, betrays that she has pent-up resentment against her niece. This discovery results in preparations for a more stringently circumscribed stay at her Aunt Pedigree's house, 'a scene of constraint'. Lumpkin is kept at home, too, and deprived of the opportunity to escape an impending marriage with Constance by a lie on his mother's part. She has given him a false age. These two characters, intended by Mrs Hardcastle for each other in marriage, are kept by circumstance and deceit in 'Liberty-hall' – in itself a strange irony. By the conclusion of the play Constance is free to leave the house not only with George Hastings, but also with her fortune, and Lumpkin is 'his own man again' in as much as he is free, presumably to marry Bet Bouncer or anyone else of his choice.

4.6 A MIRROR OF THE TIMES

We must leave these literary ideas and consider the reflection of Georgian England which is to be seen in *She Stoops to Conquer*. To an eighteenth-century audience these glimpses of aspects of everyday life helped to root the play in reality, and gave the spectators a feeling of security and identification. A difficulty that the passage of time imposes is that the everyday has now become social history and the same responses are no longer made automatically.

Town and Country

Early in the play Goldsmith comments on the dichotomy expressed in town and country living. London was the centre of fashionable society, in which the facilities offered by the two large patent theatres could be enjoyed, as well as the attractions of assemblies and dances and the intimate intellectual atmosphere offered by clubs and coffee houses. Distanced from its attractions, Hardcastle views the passing fashions as 'vanity and affectation'; his own taste is for his large country mansion and for time spent with old friends and old books. It is Mrs Hardcastle who wishes to engage much more in London society. Improvements in both the stage coaches and the roads meant faster travel, and visits to town could be undertaken more frequently. England was intersected by a series of routes which enabled one to travel by stage coach at a rate of up to sixty miles on a fine day, reduced in the wet weather, when roads became muddy and rutted, to half that distance. However, Mrs Hardcastle was deprived of the delights of the metropolis. Her own appreciation of

London life came from the 'Scandalous Magazine', possibly a reference to the *Town and Country Magazine* which carried articles, book and theatre reviews as well as society notes and gossip. She speaks of the 'tête-à-têtes', or silhouettes of well-known personalities, which decorated the periodical and were often accompanied by a text composed mainly of gossip. Something of her ignorance of society life is shown in such chance remarks as her longing to go to the Borough, the site of the infamous and disreputable Southwark Fair. It is left to Marlow to speak later with authority on the personnel of the fashionable Ladies Club or Paphian Society.

Goldsmith gives the audience hints of London society seen through the eyes of Mrs Hardcastle and Marlow. He also paints a picture of the rural neighbourhood by means of remarks of Hardcastle, Lumpkin and his rustic friends. Unflattering portraits of uncouth squires vegetating in the country had been painted in earlier plays: Sir Tunbelly Clumsey is one such in the comedy *The Relapse* by Sir John Vanbrugh (1664–1726). It is Mrs Hardcastle's earnest wish that she and her husband shall not conform to this image of country living. The few remarks that Hardcaslte makes about his rural surroundings tend to be factual. Tony Lumpkin, for his part, abetted by Stingo, the landlord of 'The Three Pigeons', invents a fantastic landscape surrounding his stepfather's house, consisting of commons haunted by highwaymen, marshlands, ranges of hills, gibbet-dotted heaths; whereas from factual descriptions we learn only of the nearby alehouse, the stables, the horsepond, and Hardcastle's house decorated with antlers standing at the top of the hill. Is there any point in Lumpkin's fabrications? This would be a matter for conjecture. One suggestion is that Lumpkin's imagination is the prop of the mainplot (the fictional inn) and an important element in the sub-plot (rescuing the jewels and Mrs Hardcastle's circular ride). Tony Lumpkin plans what is to happen in the plot and sub-plot and then becomes the catalytic force in instigating the action that follows. Thus it is that to some extent the play, both the action and the surrounding landscape, is seen through his eyes. It is for this reason that Goldsmith originally considered giving the comedy the title of *The Novel*, admittedly an uninspired choice, but nevertheless an indication of the fiction that underlies any kind of deception.

The Englishman's Home

By implication Goldsmith presents us with a further idea in the play, and one that we can appreciate more directly today; this is concerned with the Englishman's home as his castle. In the earlier years of the eighteenth century large, important houses were being built: Sir John Vanbrugh was responsible for Castle Howard in Yorkshire and William Kent (1684–1748) for Holkham Hall in Norfolk amongst other building that was undertaken. Landed families were also altering the layout of their grounds into a studied, but usually informal, countryside of lake, woodlands, grotto, hermit's cave and cascade. By the middle of the century this enthusiasm for reshaping had spread to the less affluent squires, and the Hardcastle family is no exception in undertaking 'improvements' which they view with interest as the work proceeds. It follows, therefore, that the intrusion of a seemingly unmannerly young man is all the more disruptive when a pride is taken not only in the house and its garden, but also in the ordering of life within these. Although Hardcastle's servants are gauche, he does at least attempt to improve the quality of their service at table. This is devalued by Marlow's high-handed ordering of supper and his checking of the rooms.

Arranged Marriage

Two minor reflections of eighteenth-century social custom may be mentioned briefly. These are arranged marriages and the distinctiveness of class. Of the first, Goldsmith presents us with a view which has changed considerably since he wrote the play. The courtship of Marlow and Kate has been arranged by the two fathers, Richard Hardcastle and Sir Charles. Untypically both of the young people view the match with equanimity. There are many plays of the period in which the couples revolt against the prospect. Marriages of this nature were often arranged with some kind of financial benefit to one or both of the parties; sometimes, for example, a minor titled family which had become impoverished would marry into an untitled but monied family. There is a reflection of this here in part of a conversation between the two fathers, although, as they emphasise, the match is based on their own friendship:

HARDCASTLE: . . . this union of our families will make our personal friendship hereditary; and tho' my daughter's fortune is but small . . .

SIR CHARLES: Why, Dick, will you talk of fortune to *me*? My son is possessed of more than a competence already, and can want nothing but a good and virtuous girl to share his happiness and increase it.

Hardcastle and his daughter Kate would seem to be following sensibly the aphorism of Matthew Boulton, the eighteenth-century manufacturer: 'Don't marry for money, but marry where money is.'

Class Distinction

In *She Stoops to Conquer* we see also something of the distinctiveness of various classes. Squire Hardcastle possesses an estate and thereby keeps servants; we are introduced to several of these and it soon becomes obvious that there is an easy relationship between the squire and his employees. We are introduced, too, to some of the villagers who, judging by their local form of speech, we might take to be labourers, although we know that the exciseman and the horse doctor are in the group. Tony Lumpkin, the son of a squire, transcends any class barrier in his friendship with these cronies, although for their part they show a deference towards him. Marlow is sharply conscious of differences between himself and the patrons of 'The Three Pigeons' – although in his conversation with Lumpkin he addresses him as 'Sir', his manner is sharp and his retorts brusque. This awareness of class distinction becomes an important part of the plot when he mistakes Kate for the barmaid, and, even on learning that she is related to the family, albeit as the poor relationship, he is enough aware of the social gap between them to be able to remain master of the situation. On the other hand his class consciousness does not distance him from Hastings who, although he moves with an easy assurance amongst all of the other characters in the play, appears to have little wealth. It is Constance, harping on the help her fortune would be to their marriage, who points up this fact.

4.7 TAILPIECE

This play, then, is about an amusing plot in which deception plays a part; it, too, is about the effects on people of deceptions that, in the main, are kindly meant; it is about an understanding of the philosophical implications of deception and the discovery of the truth; it is in turn a model by means of which Goldsmith illustrates his theory of what he believes comedy to be about.

5 TECHNICAL FEATURES

5.1 THE FORM AND STRUCTURE OF THE PLAY

The Derivatory Nature of the Play

She Stoops to Conquer is the story of the trials that separate two contrasting pairs of romantic lovers, of their warming towards each other, and of their final happiness. Such characters in such a progression are far from original. Playwrights since the days of the Athenian writer Menander (342-292 BC) have used similar plots. There is, too, Goldsmith's lack of originality in selecting the kernel of his play. The plot is partly based on his own youthful experience in mistaking Squire Featherstone's house for an inn and partly on the plot of a play by Pierre Marivaux (1688-1763) entitled *Le Jeu de L'Amour et du Hasard*. In his biography of Goldsmith, Lytton Sells suggests that the encounters between Marlow and Kate are based on the meetings of Isabelle and tongue-tied Philiste in *Le Glorieux* by Philippe Destouches (1680-1754). Nor are Goldsmith's characters original. Some are based on members of his family (as, for example, Mrs Hardcastle who is possibly a reflection of the playwright's own mother), and some are derived from earlier literary characters. However, the strength of Goldsmith's work lies in the warmth and humanity with which he has infused his characters; his own genuine enjoyment of the plot which makes it more than an interacting mechanism and his hope that in all the situations his audiences will be given opportunities for laughter and amusement.

The Sub-plot

The inclusion of a sub-plot in a comedy was unusual in Goldsmith's day. In *She Stoops to Conquer* the story of the romance and intended elopement of Constance and Hastings forms the substance of this. The activities of the two characters form an interesting point of comparison with the principal lovers.

The Five-Act Structure

In common with many plays of Goldsmith's day *She Stoops to Conquer* is structured in five acts.

The first act is in the nature of an introduction. An audience at the theatre is able to see the location in which the play takes place. The date of the play is established; an audience at the opening night in 1773 realised that the time was the then present. Most important, the principal characters are introduced. In the second scene of this act the device on which the play hangs, Tony Lumpkin's deception and the mistake of Marlow and Hastings in taking Hardcastle's house for an inn, is established.

The second act is a development of the seminal ideas planted in Act 1. It consists of the two parties, the inhabitants of Hardcastle's house and the stranded travellers, meeting and the embarrassments caused in this. The two pairs of lovers also meet for the first time on stage. In the meeting of Hastings and Constance the plan to elope is broached which forms the substance of the sub-plot.

In a five-act structure the third act often presents the audience with some kind of watershed, a way in which the attention of the audience is redirected to the piece. Such occurs in both the main plot and the sub-plot: in the former Kate determines that Marlow will become her husband; in the latter Constance is at the point of elopement, with her jewels safely subtracted from her aunt. Each situation is a comment on the other and much depends on the determination of the two young women involved.

The fourth act is one in which, having almost achieved their objective, complications bar the way to fulfilment and happiness for the romantic leads: Marlow is ordered to leave Hardcastle's house and Hastings' elopement is thwarted by Mrs Hardcastle's determination to remove her niece from the house. Again, in this exodus, parallel situations are presented. In the sub-plot, just as it seems that all of the preparations for the elopement have been successfully accomplished, there is a reversal when Mrs Hardcastle discovers the contents of Hastings' letter. Such letters, making or marring a situation, have been a common device in both tragedies and comedies since Shakespeare's day and were a feature of a number of eighteenth-century plays.

The fifth act is one of resolution: the difficulties both sets of lovers have encountered are resolved and a promise is made of security and happiness to come. An impression of the reward of virtue and the punishment of folly is suggested.

This five-act structure helps to determine the form of the play.

5.2   THE UNITY OF THE PLAY

Unity of Place

A further determinant is the utilisation of a unity of time, place and action. This was a convention established in Greek plays of the fifth century BC. In Goldsmith's day it was not used to any great extent in comedies. Some writers, though, favoured this additional discipline. Richard Brinsley Sheridan, the author of *The Rivals* (staged in 1775) favoured applying two of the laws of unity. His piece was set in a single town, encompassing the span of a day. Goldsmith was more rigorous. *She Stoops to Conquer*, with the exception of two scenes, is confined to the Great Chamber of an old-fashioned house, and even when departing from this room, the writer keeps his scene within the confines of the village. Changes of location brought variety to a play. Goldsmith therefore has to compensate for this by providing a range of situations which generate humour and interest. This is one good reason for providing the play with the unfashionable, and in this case, extended, sub-plot.

Units of Time

The sub-title *The Mistakes of a Night* fixes the limits of the time-span: It is early evening when the play opens, and, although a two-hour time-lapse occurs between Acts 4 and 5 during which Mrs Hardcastle takes her ride, the family have yet to have supper when the curtain falls. Goldsmith envisaged a time span of little more than five hours.

Unity of Action

Unity of action demands that no material superfluous to the play is introduced. The action of the sub-plot is carefully dovetailed into the action of the mainplot so that in this combination any suggestion of extraneous incidents is avoided. Several eighteenth-century writers, however, criticised Goldsmith for a breach of this rule as well as for a lack of probability in selecting the incidents which go to make up the plot. For example, both the extended deception about Hardcastle's house and Lumpkin's deception in getting Mrs Hardcastle to believe she was forty miles from home when she was, in fact, at the bottom of her own garden were condemned as highly improbable. So too was the over-easy device of deceiving Lumpkin about his true age. This a writer in the *Monthly Review* considered to be 'lugged in, the most violently, of any things we ever remember to have either read or seen'. Another writer, this time in the *London Chronicle*, was of the opinion that 'the Circumstance of the Change of Dress was dragged in, on purpose to give the Lady a more plausible Pretext of passing upon her Lover as a Barmaid'. Obviously individual people, now as much as in the eighteenth century, will have differing ideas about the merit of these strictures.

5.3 THE PRINCIPAL CHARACTERS

Class Distinction

The characters in *She Stoops to Conquer* belong to two social classes. These are the minor gentry and the villagers. Hardcastle is the squire of the village, and Tony Lumpkin's natural father was 'old Squire Lumpkin' with his collection of 'horses, dogs and girls'. Marlow, for his part, is an equal match socially for Hardcastle's daughter, as his father is a titled gentleman. There is, therefore, a parity of class amongst the principal characters. The villagers form the 'low' or rustic contrast and are an invaluable source of humour, whether they are Hardcastle's servants who are kept out of sight the greater part of the time, or the village locals at 'The Three Pigeons'.

Names of the Characters

Whether they are people of high or low estate many of the characters in the play have names which reflect personality. Hardcastle's name encompasses the idea that an Englishman's home is his castle and he won't brook intrusions. Tony Lumpkin's name, with its similarity to 'bumpkin', reminds us that, on the face of it, he is a rural simpleton. However, there is more to his character than that; Miss Neville's first name, Constance, points to the engaging quality which prompts her to keep her tryst with George Hastings.

Of several of the minor characters who appear on stage, only Diggory has a rural name. Those, however, who are mentioned in the dialogue enjoy a range of humorous names. Mrs Oddfish (the curate's wife); Cripplegate (the dancing master who is lame); Farmer Murrain (this is the eighteenth-century term for the cattle plague, foot and mouth disease) are a few examples. There are, too, the names of the members of the Ladies Club which Marlow attends. That of Mrs Mantrap reflects her character obviously and Lady Betty Blackleg may be a reference to Mrs Montagu and her friends, who formed a literary society in the 1750s which was called by Admiral Boscawen the 'Blue Stocking Society'. Miss Biddy Buckskin is the wise change of name for Rachael Lloyd, who was one of the original members of the Paphian Society.

Although in their names Goldsmith emphasises certain traits, the characters in his play are not flat, pasteboard types. They abound in details which give them an engaging interest, and a stage life. We must remember, however, that in delineating them Goldsmith is not seeking a realistic approach. The characters are the stock ones of comedy and as such are cogs in the elaborate mechanism of the plot. In order to give them a memorable life in the short span of the play Goldsmith legitimately draws exaggerated features, and it is in the ensuing confrontations, one with another, of these that much of the humour of the situation resides.

Squire Richard Hardcastle

Richard Hardcastle is a member of the English squirearchy: he owns a mansion, an amount of land around it, and a number of servants to work in the house and on the land. Such men as Hardcastle were the backbone of England in the eighteenth century, and had often been portrayed in various literary forms. Squire Allworthy of Allworthy Hall, in the novel *Tom Jones* by Joseph Fielding (1707–54), is a precursor of Squire Hardcastle. One of the earliest points made to the audience about him is that he is conservative, and in this he was true to form.

The tract writer Hannah More (1745-1833) described the traditionalist squire:

> He dreaded nought like alteration,
> Improvement still was innovation.

Hardcastle has a penchant for all things old - 'old friends, old times, old manners, old books, old wine'. Goldsmith, himself, was a conservative person and unashamedly shows his admiration for men like Hardcastle.

When Marlow and Hastings arrive at Hardcastle's house the master tells them: 'This is Liberty-hall, gentlemen. You may do just as you please here'. Interestingly Goldsmith picks up a remark (*hi sunt liberae aedes*) spoken by Pleusicles in *Miles Gloriosus*, a comedy by the Roman playwright Titus Maccius Plautus (250-184 BC). Hardcastle is (like Shakespeare's Falstaff) drawn in the tradition of the Old Soldier. His conversation is full of stories of campaigns in which he has served and the famous generals he has known. At times mistakes are made in these narrations and the audience is led to wonder to what extent Hardcastle was at the heart of the campaign. A further drawback is that in the accounting of these legends Hardcastle becomes boring to all but the most rustic of servants.

'Liberty Hall' is a fair description of Hardcastle's generous hospitality. He provides a sumptuous supper for Marlow on his arrival. He expects his hospitality to be treated with respect and gratitude, however, and when Marlow behaves boorishly he is rightly disturbed and discusses the fellow's response with Kate.

In his kindly tolerance of his second wife and her son, Hardcastle's own strength of character is revealed. In spite of being a traditionalist he tolerates Dorothy's somewhat pathetic attempts to be fashionable and to grasp back her lost years. He has a kindly indulgence, too, of Lumpkin, although he is cognizant of the fellow's self-seeking and wastrel behaviour. He is keen, however, to ensure that Tony is given his freedom to renounce any intention of marrying Constance when his wife deceives the lad about his true age. He has a liberal attitude towards his own daughter, allowing her to make her own choice of husband without abnegating his responsibility to provide her with that choice. He tolerates, too, her fondness for 'superfluous silk' in which she goes visiting, and the two have worked out a compromise in which Kate wears somewhat plain clothes in the evening and silks by day. In this arrangement we can guess at the respect as well as affection in which he is held by his daughter.

Although outraged by Marlow's behaviour, and finally attempting to send him packing, he is gracious enough, once he knows of Marlow's mistake, to see the underlying humour, and gleefully recounts this to his old friend, Sir Charles Marlow.

We know nothing of the physical characteristics Goldsmith envisaged Hardcastle possessing; but the actor who first played the part, Edward Shuter, was a florid, overweight personage who died three years after instigating the role. The heavy presence he gave to Squire Hardcastle would be given verification by Sir Horace Walpole (1717-97): looking at the squires of Norfolk he referred to them as 'mountains of roast beef' and it is in that mould that Hardcastle was first cast.

Mrs Dorothy Hardcastle

Mrs Hardcastle is the least attractive person in the play. Her basic faults are her greed and her lack of generosity. To a man of Goldsmith's impulsive generosity these must have seemed serious defects of character. She is the custodian of her niece's jewellery: one of her interests in attempting to marry Constance to her son, Tony Lumpkin, is to keep the fortune in the family; when Constance legitimately asks for the jewels, she tries to fob her off with her own unfashionable garnets, decoration for an older woman; and when Constance appeals for her fortune to the good nature of her guardian after her return from the aborted elopement, her words meet with dismissal by Mrs Hardcastle. It is, indeed, the elopement which stings the woman to an uncharacteristic burst of decisive activity; she immediately decides to lodge her niece with her Aunt Pedigree.

Deceit is another fault from which Mrs Hardcastle suffers. Her deceit about her own age is merely a form of vanity in her dalliance with Hastings: her deceit about Tony's age is, as we have seen, more seriously connected with her desire to hold on to Constance's fortune for as long as possible.

In her relations with her son she vacillates between idolisation on the one hand, giving the impression that in the past the wayward youth has been irremediably spoilt; whilst on the other hand she suddenly turns on him referring to him as 'monster' or 'viper'. In spoiling him she has managed to persuade herself that they boy is a sickly youth whom she must protect. To be fair she makes every effort to stop the 'highwayman' from perpetrating the worst of her fears and murdering her son, offering herself as a victim in his place. But all this is a form of foolishness. Her own continuous nagging has little effect on her son and her sarcasm is lost on her niece when the plans for the elopement are laid bare.

Her attempts at fashionableness are a further form of foolishness; there is little chance that the villagers to whom reference is made would appreciate the finer points of either Mrs Hardcastle's appearance or her chatter. It would seem probable that the alteration to the house and the grounds, 'the improvements', are carried out at her instigation, rather than that of Hardcastle. Little indication in the play is given about their suitability; obviously they are grafted on to the existing mansion, rather than forming an integral act of rebuilding.

For Mrs Hardcastle Hastings' letter, which she reads to the assembled company, is one means of realising the light she is seen in by others: '. . . the *hag* (ay the hag) your mother . . .'. Perspicacity, either in realising the truth about herself or about others, is a gift in which Mrs Hardcastle is lacking.

In many ways Mrs Hardcastle resembles Mrs Primrose in Goldsmith's novel *The Vicar of Wakefield*, a portrait thought to be based on the writer's own mother, who was a matchmaker, but possibly needed to be, in attempting to settle her daughters. The part of Mrs Hardcastle was played in the first production by a highly experienced actress, Jane Green, who also established herself in the roles of Mrs Malaprop in *The Rivals* and the Nurse in *Romeo and Juliet*. In Thomas Parkinson's painting of the 'highwayman' scene she is portrayed as a dumpy, overpainted person.

Tony Lumpkin

Boobies whose fathers over-indulged them are quite common in seventeenth-century literature; those with foolishly fond mothers are rare, and so in some ways Goldsmith's conception of Tony Lumpkin is a new creation. However, Lumpkin does have several literary precursors. The two principal ones are Humphrey Gubbin in *The Tender Husband* by Richard Steele and Young Hartford in *The Lancashire Witches* by the playwright Thomas Shadwell (1642?-92). Humphrey Gubbin is 'a pert blockhead, and very lively'; like Tony he is kept in ignorance of the fact that he has come of age. A further similarity is that he aids Clermont, the young hero, in his courtship. The actions of Tony recall those of the earlier rustic. Young Hartford bears similarity with Tony in as much as he is a clownish squireling who by night misleads two London gentleman, Bellfort and Doubty, to the house of Sir Edward, his father. Thus the framework of *She Stoops to Conquer* is closely paralleled by that of *The Lancashire Witches*.

Many sixteenth and seventeenth-century comedies contain a mischievous, Puck-like character. As with Puck in *A Midsummer Night's Dream* an important purpose of such characters is to set the action working. Tony Lumpkin is the prime mover of the plot; he initiates the mistakes of the night by misdirecting Marlow and Hastings; he is a key figure in both the frustrated elopement and the attempted recovery of Constance's fortune; his ultimate prank, leading Mrs Hardcastle and Constance on a circular journey instead of to Constance's Aunt Pedigree and finally leaving the coach stranded in the horse-pond, safely brings Constance and Hastings together permanently.

This play is one of disguise and mistaken identity, and in this business Lumpkin helps to shape the disguises of other people. In the eyes of Marlow and Hastings he disguises Hardcastle as an innkeeper. So much has his joke preyed on her that for Mrs Hardcastle her husband is temporarily disguised as a highwayman and she projects her own dishonest attempts to attain a fortune onto him. Lumpkin and his friends create a disguised countryside for some people too: for Marlow and Hastings as well as for Constance and Mrs Hardcastle; both sets of characters are travellers at the time at which they are misled along Lumpkin's fantasy routes. In getting people to misidentify each other, revenge is a strong driving force. In 'The Three Pigeons' Lumpkin is annoyed with his stepfather for constantly disparaging him as a blockhead and he realises he 'could be so revenged upon the old grumble-tonian'. A double opportunity to score greets him when he is accosted in patronising tones by the London travellers. He resents his mother's interference in both her matchmaking and in her attempting to deprive him of his liberty by keeping him tied to the house his stepfather refers to as 'Liberty-hall'. All three parties underrate Lumpkin: they refer to him in specific ways as a country simpleton; he has, in fact, the wit to engineer the principal situations of the piece.

There is little opportunity with so short a time-span as a single night for characters to develop to any degree: Marlow and Lumpkin are the exceptions. At the beginning of the play Lumpkin is by repute a lazy wastrel and this seems to be confirmed on his first appearance in which he presents himself as the ale-house quaffer. But there is more to Lumpkin than that. There is a measure of rural conservatism in Tony Lumpkin, for in him the local rustics see a mirror of his father's country skills; and rural traditionalism was something for which Goldsmith stood, as his poem *The Deserted Village* demonstrates. A scorn for reading and learning, a jibe at the Methodist preacher's abhorrence of alcohol and an honest lusting after Bet Bouncer are an exemplification of Lumpkin's traditional slot in rural life. It is when the elopement plot has been discovered and before the deserting pair are off the premises that Lumpkin reveals his true colours in his ability to transcend petty squabbles and bring a failure to the point of success. The incisiveness of his decision to please himself is quickly and determinedly put to the service and pleasure of others. In his dictum '. . . we kiss and be friends . . .' is a workable philosophy; in putting it to the test he reveals himself a gentleman at least, and more than a low figure of amusement.

Goldsmith uses Tony to set up one of his most humorous and also elegantly constructed scenes in the careful preplanning for that in which Constance's jewels are 'stolen', and the double understanding that is in Tony's affirmation, 'I can bear witness'. In this we see most clearly not only Goldsmith's creation of a lively, fun-loving character who can twist words and situations to suit his own purposes, but also the way in which the playwright uses each of his characters as a cog in the mechanism of the plot. The only danger is that Goldsmith may be creating too elaborate a joke, needing a kind of prescience that is uncharacteristic of his character. Each member of the audience has to make up his own mind about that.

The role of Tony Lumpkin was played by a slightly known actor, John Quick, who rose to eminence in the Georgian theatre as a popular, if sometimes vulgar, comedian. Parkinson's painting shows a very lively impersonation of the role in which the actor wears a ridiculously elaborately embroidered waistcoat, pointing to the fact that humour may lie in excess. The critic of the *Morning Chronicle* found the character an engaging and amusing one:

The Squire is a compound of whim and good-natured mischief; the engine of the plot, and the source of infinite mirth and a variety of very laughable mistakes . . .

Marlow

The part of Marlow, the role of the male lover, is a highly conventional one. From the days of late Athenian comedy, lovers such as he had cleared away the growth of parental opposition and social intervention until the landscape was clear to propose marriage to their heroines. As a stock type he affects the stock vices and virtues of the lover: he takes himself seriously, and thus is easy to trick; he knows his rightful place in a society conscious of a class structure; he willingly accedes to the social conventions of an arranged marriage, although here the arrangements are more liberal than was sometimes the case; and when he discovers a young lady to whom he can respond he pursues her with steadfastness, although Marlow is a typical eighteenth-century lover in eschewing overt enthusiasm.

Marlow differs in two respects from the stock lover. Firstly he is unduly easy to gull, and secondly he has a strangely divided response to women of his own social standing and to his inferiors. In the course of the play everybody, except Mrs Hardcastle, tricks Marlow at some point: Tony and Kate deceive him with their extended pranks; Hastings and Constance maintain deceptions; and Hardcastle and Sir Charles lead him to believe he is alone with Kate when they are hidden behind the screen. The whole play hangs on the thread of deception – and Marlow is the main victim. There is little in the man, apart from his seriousness (and even here Marlow is, by repute, a veritable rattle once he gets to the Paphian Society), to mark him out as a fellow who is made to be duped. Nor are the characters who trick him seen in a reprehensible light.

More strange is Marlow's divided response to women. As with the gulling this is in part no more than a necessity of the plot. Nevertheless Goldsmith is presenting us with more than ciphers in this character. In his over-reaction to women of his own social status Marlow acts as a parody of the hero of a sentimental drama. A convenient comparison would be with the parody of another situation, the response of

Faulkland to Julia in *The Rivals*. Marlow is over-sensitive to Kate's responses to him – but Goldsmith exaggerates this defect to a ridiculous degree. In order to preserve the amusement of this situation the playwright has to limit the encounters between Marlow and Kate or the humour will become dissipated. Hence it is useful to introduce Marlow to Kate in differing *personae* – as the barmaid and poor relation of the family. But this limitation is also used in order to advance the plot. Not only does a romance develop between Marlow and the poor relation, but this development allows the activities of Marlow to be seen through two pairs of eyes, Hardcastle's and Kate's, and to each his behaviour appears quite different. Although Goldsmith uses it merely as a convention, in Marlow's differing attitudes to women of high or low degree we sense a legacy of Restoration comedy: women are a necessary satisfaction for, and easy prey to, men's desires. We may, perhaps, compare Marlow with Horner in *The Country Wife*, a comedy by William Wycherley (1640–1716). Horner (his name implies a cuckolder) seduces women in order to gratify himself and, incidentally, them; but more important, through the seductions he establishes his essential male quality in the society within which he moves.

In further ways Marlow appears in differing lights to various people. To George Hastings he is a staunchly loyal friend; he makes the long and uncomfortable journey to Hardcastle's territory principally in order to introduce Hastings to the family in which he is as yet unknown. It is ironical that in this family Hastings creates the good impression and Marlow the bad. To Hardcastle, Marlow is a boorish fellow, imperious in his commands and impatient with Hardcastle's military anecdotes. His effect on Kate to start with is uncertain. She realises that if she can penetrate his bashfulness there is something 'pretty well', and after the encounter in her disguise she tells her father that Marlow possesses 'only the faults that will pass off with time and the virtues that will improve with age . . . '.

Commenting on this creation of Goldsmith's the critic in the *Morning Chronicle* found Marlow a wholly acceptable character: 'Mr. Marlow, a man of sense [ie sensibility], education and breeding . . .. This character is, as far as we can recollect, an original one.' By the latter remark the reviewer infers that he is not based on similar characters in other plays as, for example, is Tony Lumpkin. We have already seen, however, that he is drawn in the stock portraiture of the traditional romantic hero. If not from literature, there may well be elements from life encapsulated in Marlow. It is possible to see something of Goldsmith himself here: he was duped by a joker into lodging at Ardagh House supposing it to be an inn; he was a stylish person who enjoyed dressing well; and his poverty had probably kept him from the society of women of his own social status during the earlier part of his life.

George Hastings

Hastings is a contrast to Marlow, although as both men are light, romantic heroes the opportunities for dramatic contrasts are limited. He has a social smoothness and, when somewhat rarely annoyed, an aggressiveness which Marlow lacks. His own established romance with Constance forms the subplot to the play and it is a foil to the developing romance of Marlow with Kate.

Hastings is genuinely in love with Constance Neville. He accompanies Marlow to Hardcastle's house in order to gain admittance and put his preconceived plan for an elopement into operation. There is no hint of fortune seeking in his proposal – indeed Hastings is prepared to leave for France without any of the jewellery Constance has inherited, and he reiterates this several times. However, an elopement is a clandestine and, to some extent, an unworthy subterfuge (an example of deception in a play suffused with it) and Hastings develops in as much as at the end of the play he is prepared to make a speech of apology to Hardcastle for the unworthiness of such an intention.

He works on the Hardcastles with a social smoothness. He plays Mrs Hardcastle's game, flattering her when necessary and indulging her with gossip of London fashions. Although Hardcastle becomes over-wrought about Marlow's behaviour, he is able to accept that of Hastings without offence. Even when Mrs Hardcastle ultimately discovers Hastings' letter outlining the plan for the elopement she does not rail at him by name. He has, then, made as good an impression on the elderly couple as the circumstances will allow.

When stung to anger he can turn on Tony Lumpkin and yet at the same time deal in a cool and dignified way with Marlow's remonstrations for misleading him about the inn. Well organised in his planning, it is somewhat uncharacteristic of him to send, foolishly, Constance's jewels to Marlow as soon as they come into his hands. This action surprises Marlow. In returning the jewels to the 'landlady' Marlow hoists the plotting Hastings with his own petard.

More astute than Marlow, socially at ease, determined in his purposes, eloquent, in all these respects Hastings makes a good foil to the principal romantic role.

Kate Hardcastle

Kate is presented as a refined contrast to her rustic, rumbustious step-brother. In society she is highly competent, a fact which is illustrated in her first meeting with Marlow, indeed, she has spent 'a year or two in town' according to her father, which has given her assurance. The first impression Kate makes on the audience is of a dutiful and submissive daughter: obediently she accedes to her father's request that she should wear plain clothes in the evenings. Quickly we learn, however, that Kate has astutely learned to manipulate the situation so that it is possible for her to wear elaborate clothes during the day when she goes visiting. Who she visited thus formally in the village as Goldsmith paints it is hard to envisage. Similarly she dutifully agrees not only to meet Marlow but also to like him; but again we learn in the following act that Kate is going to use this situation to further her own purposes. The rather dull virtue of dutifulness is brightened by her own inventive powers.

In her initial approach to Marlow Kate is modest; moreover she is highly accomplished in her attempts to create something positive from the encounter. As Marlow will not take the initiative in pressing his claim, she quickly perceives ways in which she can draw him out. This perspicacity is one of Kate's great advantages in her relationships with other people. She even manages to live in peace with her stepmother and stepbrother.

Goldsmith takes no moral stand about disguise and deception; it can either be used wrongfully (as Tony uses it, for reasons of revenge, in Act 1) or rightly. The latter Kate does in assuming the role of barmaid and poor relation, because through her disguise she helps Marlow to discover in himself the ability to unify his bashful and his precocious natures. Eventually, of course, this is to her own advantage, when Marlow finally manages to propose to Kate as his social equal.

Mrs Bulkeley took on the role of Kate. 'The Author could hardly have wished for a better representative', said the critic of the *Morning Chronicle*.

Constance Neville

A person who does not regard the Hardcastle household as Liberty Hall is Constance. Although her father approved of George Hastings as a husband for his daughter, since her bereavement Constance has been forced to 'stoop to dissimulation to avoid oppression' and pretend that she loves her cousin, Lumpkin. The sub-plot is the tale of Hastings' attempt to free Constance from the custody of her aunt. In order to achieve any kind of freedom Constance has to dissemble on several fronts: she leads her aunt to imagine that she loves Tony; she attempts several minor ruses in order to regain the fortune left to her by her uncle; she is part of the deception in making Marlow believe he is staying at an inn; and she has to pretend that life is normal, without the promise of the impending flight to France.

Her attitude towards her fortune is a more practical one than Hastings adopts. She realises that the capital can be a security in their future life together, and she shows considerable determination in attempting to wrest the jewels from her aunt's grasp and in appealing to her uncle's tenderness for their recovery.

Her nature is summed up in her name. For months before the start of the play she has remained constant to George Hastings and when her aunt attempts to remove her to her Aunt Pedigree's house she puns on her own name, exhorting George to wait in constancy for three years until she is of age.

In many Georgian plays (and indeed earlier ones dating back to Shakespeare's comedies) the heroine is accompanied by a sometimes pale companion. Constance fulfils this role. Goldsmith scores, however, in giving Constance a well-defined character of her own and contrasting this, as well as her situation, with that of Kate. As a foil to Kate's liveliness and imaginative creativity Constance is firmly level-headed and faithful.

In considering the characters in *She Stoops to Conquer* we see that Goldsmith works within several frames of reference. Nearly all of the characters relate to stock types because the progression of the play is the classical one of young lovers passing through various family difficulties until they arrive at a point of happiness. Thus the two pairs of lovers correspond to stock types, and the figures of the Hardcastles similarly so. Additionally some of the characters derive from literary sources; with these Goldsmith reworks traditional material. We see then that the playwright is not working with portraits drawn from life. It is a mark of his skilfulness that these stock and literary types are infused with life and interest, so that in watching a performance the audience is led to believe that they exhibit qualities of naturalness.

5.4 LANGUAGE

The Language of the Educated

> . . . when [Goldsmith] has thrust his people into a situation, he makes them talk very *funnily*. His merit is that sort of dialogue which lies on a level with the most common understandings; and in that low mischief and mirth which we laugh at, while we are ready to despise ourselves for so doing.

This is part of a notice of *She Stoops to Conquer* from the *Monthly Review* for March 1773. In the main it is unfavourable in its comments, but the language of the play is amusing, and commended on that score.

On first hearing the language the audience is misled to imagine that it has qualities of spontaneity and naturalness; whereas in reality Goldsmith carefully writes in a number of language registers, adjusting these carefully to suit each of the speakers. Although, too, the language seems to flow effortlessly, some of it is highly artificial and formal, and so there is this attribute to consider as well.

In our first meeting with Hardcastle we become aware of his mannerism of prefacing many of his sentences with an 'Ay'. He also tends to pick up a key word in each of his wife's speeches and build his next sentence around that. Thus, Mrs Hardcastle remarks 'You must allow the boy a little humour' and Hardcastle fastens on 'allow' in order to turn the point against her: 'I'd sooner allow him an horse-pond.' He has a further characteristic of formally building up lists, as though a multiplicity of instances will prove a point: 'I love every thing that's old : old friends, old times, old manners, old books, old wine . . . '.

His wife's speech tends to be littered with tags and aphorisms which, in her own way, she often uses against her husband: 'You may be a Darby, but I'll be no Joan, I promise you.' There is often an unpleasant moralising in these remarks, especially when Mrs Hardcastle is in the wrong. For example, about Constance's jewels, she tells the girl : '. . . tho' we lose our fortune, yet we should not lose our patience'. Under extreme provocation this mannered style forsakes her. To a thwarted Lumpkin she bawls: 'And you, you great ill-fashioned oaf, with scarce enough sense to keep your mouth shut. Were you too join'd against me?'

Kate tends to be formal in her language. At her first meeting with Marlow her speech becomes highly patterned in order to contrast with his breakdown of language, and also with her own terse asides to the audience. In speaking of Marlow to her father she does so in terms of a formally ordered set of clauses:

He treated me with diffidence and respect; censured the manners of the age; admired the prudence of girls that never laughed; tired me with apologies for being tiresome; then left the room with a bow, and, madam, I would not for the world detain you.

Hardcastle's speech immediately following picks up this patterning, but his meaning is the antithesis of hers. Significantly the form of the language draws our attention to the fact that we are presented with two contrasting views of Marlow.

The sentences of Kate the barmaid tend to be terse and to the point; they differ from speeches made in her own person. Occasionally she introduces a coined word in order to suggest rustic speech: 'obstropalous' is one such, obviously related to 'obstreperous'.

Marlow's use of language depends on whom he is addressing. With male social inferiors he is brusque to the point of rudeness, as in his interchange with Lumpkin in Act 1. Meeting Kate for the first time, sequential patterns of language break down completely and she has to build his sentences for him. With female social inferiors he at once becomes expansive, a little patronising and something of a raconteur, as, for example, when he describes the Paphian Society to the 'barmaid' – hardly a subject in which she would show much interest. When he discovers his mistake in presuming the house to be an inn, instead of a blustering annoyance, he speaks in mannered prose as he tells Kate: 'I mistook your assiduity for assurance, and your simplicity for allurement.'

Rustic language

Goldsmith, in commenting on the dialogue in *Douglas* by John Home, wrote of the shepherd's language: 'It requires some art to dress the thoughts and phrases of the common people, without letting them swell into bombast, or sink into vulgarity.' Fifteen years after writing that sentence Goldsmith was creating the rustic language of Lumpkin, Stingo, Diggory and Ralph. In order to point up Lumpkin's rural background the oath 'Ecod' is peppered over speeches, reinforced by similes of country life: 'She has as many tricks as a hare in a thicket . . .'. In order to avoid charges of vulgarity little deviation from the norm of Georgian speech is made in the dialogue of this important character. But for those characters who appear for only short periods the language is more obviously rustic and there is an indication of pronunciation in such spelling as 'bekeays' for 'because'. In the rustic dialogue at 'The Three Pigeons' there are substitutions of coined words for the conventional; sentences begin with such constructions as 'If so be that . . .'; and a low tone pervades the content as when, speaking of old Squire Lumpkin, it was said 'he kept the best horses, dogs and girls in the whole country'. Even the yokels, though, Goldsmith uses as a mouthpiece for ironic comment. In a scene which is palpably about low life one of the fellows comments: 'O damn any thing that's *low*, I can't bear it.'

As the play progresses many of the speeches of a range of characters are coloured by irony, whether it is the irony of an on-stage situation in which the audience is informed of factors of which the characters are unaware, or an irony of tone (as in the 'low' example in the previous paragraph) or the irony implicit in parody, as when Marlow addresses Miss Hardcastle in a burlesque of the sentimental hero at a point in the play at which he is totally unheroic.

We have already observed that the characters cannot be described as 'natural' as they are drawn from literary types. The same point may be made about the language. This often consists of artificially constructed, highly formalised speeches. The glory of it is that it flows with such ease and accomplishment that in watching the play we believe the speeches of the characters to come from the heart rather than from the playwright's polished pen.

6 AN EXAMINATION OF TWO SELECTED PASSAGES

6.1 TWO ENCOUNTERS

In Marlow, Goldsmith presents us with a man who can make differing impressions on various people. Reputedly with women of low society his approach is brash and conceited, whilst with women of some social quality he is reserved, develops a stammer and can barely string a sentence together. Goldsmith presents the audience with two such encounters, and unbeknown to Marlow they are both with the same person. The first occurs in Act 2 and consists of the initial encounter between Marlow and Kate, the young woman intended to be his wife. The second interview is again with Marlow and Kate but on this occasion Marlow mistakes Kate for a barmaid on the staff of the fictitious inn; this occurs in Act 3. Obviously the interviews form a strong point of contrast and Goldsmith employs this device of a parallel incident not only to demonstrate the difference in Marlow's responses, but also in the first meeting to construct a parody of a scene in a sentimental comedy and in the second faithfully to present the audience with an instance of dialogue which points up differences in social standing. Each excerpt generates its own particular brand of humour. The quiet pleasantry of the first may have been an acceptable amusement for the patrons in the pit and boxes who were conversant with such sentimental novels as *Pamela* by Samuel Richardson (1689–1761) or with the travel journal by Laurence Sterne (1713–1768) *A Sentimental Journey*, or indeed with the numbers of sentimental dramas presented at London's two patent theatres. The humour in the second excerpt is of a broader kind, a mistake of identity, an advance, and then the very situation with which the play will ultimately finish, Kate and Marlow's joining together. It is only the circumstances which differ.

6.2 A PARODY OF SENSIBILITY

Enter MISS HARDCASTLE *as returned from walking, a Bonnet,* etc.

HASTINGS (*introducing them*): Miss Hardcastle, Mr Marlow, I'm proud of bringing two persons of such merit together, that only want to know, to esteem each other.

MISS HARDCASTLE (*aside*): Now, for meeting my modest gentleman with a demure face, and quite in his own manner. (*After a pause, in which he appears very uneasy and disconcerted*) I'm glad of your safe arrival, Sir—I'm told you had some accidents by the way.

MARLOW: Only a few madam. Yet, we had some. Yes, Madam a good many accidents, but should be sorry—Madam—or rather glad of any accidents—that are so agreeably concluded. Hem!

HASTINGS (*To him*): You never spoke better in your whole life. Keep it up, and I'll insure you the victory.

MISS HARDCASTLE: I'm afraid you flatter, Sir. You that have seen so much of the finest company can find little entertainment in an obscure corner of the country.

MARLOW (*Gathering courage*): I have lived, indeed, in the world, Madam; but I have kept very little company. I have been but an observer upon life, Madam, while others were enjoying it.

MISS NEVILLE: But that, I am told, is the way to enjoy it at last.

HASTINGS (*To him*): Cicero never spoke better. Once more, and you are confirm'd in assurance for ever.

MARLOW (*To him*): Hem! Stand by me then, and when I'm down, throw in a word or two to set me up again.

MISS HARDCASTLE: An observer, like you, upon life, were, I fear, disagreeably employed, since you must have had much more to censure than to approve.

MARLOW: Pardon me, Madam, I was always willing to be amused. The folly of most people is rather an object of mirth than uneasiness.

HASTINGS (*To him*): Bravo, Bravo. Never spoke so well in your whole life. Well! Miss Hardcastle, I see that you and Mr Marlow are going to be very good company. I believe our being here will but embarrass the interview.

MARLOW: Not in the least, Mr. Hastings. We like your company of all things. (*To him*) Zounds! George, sure you won't go? How can you leave us?

HASTINGS: Our presence will but spoil conversation, so we'll retire to the next room. (*To him*) You don't consider, man, that we are to manage a little tête-à-tête of our own.   [*Exeunt.*]

MISS HARDCASTLE (*After a pause*): But you have not been wholly an observer, I presume, Sir: The ladies I should hope have employed some part of your addresses.

MARLOW (*Relapsing into timidity*): Pardon me, Madam, I—I—I—as yet have studied—only—to—deserve them.

MISS HARDCASTLE: And that some say is the very worst way to obtain them.

MARLOW: Perhaps so, madam. But I love to converse only with the more grave and sensible part of the sex.—But I'm afraid I grow tiresome.

MISS HARDCASTLE: Not at all, Sir; there is nothing I like so much as grave conversation myself; I could hear it for ever. Indeed I have often been surprized how a man of *sentiment* could ever admire those light airy pleasures, where nothing reaches the heart.

MARLOW: It's—a disease—of the mind, madam. In the variety of tastes there must be some who, wanting a relish—for—um-a-um.

MISS HARDCASTLE: I understand you, Sir. There must be some, who wanting a relish for refined pleasures, pretend to despise what they are incapable of tasting.

MARLOW: My meaning, madam, but infinitely better expressed. And I can't help observing—a—

MISS HARDCASTLE (*Aside*): Who could ever suppose this fellow impudent upon some occasions. (*To him*) You were going to observe, Sir—

MARLOW: I was observing, madam—I protest, madam, I forget what I was going to observe.

MISS HARDCASTLE (*Aside*): I vow and so do I. (*To him*) You were observing, Sir, that in this age of hypocrisy—something about hypocrisy, Sir.

MARLOW: Yes, madam. In this age of hypocrisy there are few who upon strict enquiry do not—a—a—a—

MISS HARDCASTLE: I understand you perfectly, Sir.

MARLOW (*Aside*): Egad! and that's more than I do myself.

MISS HARDCASTLE: You mean that in this hypocritical age there are few that do not condemn in public what they practise in private, and think they pay every debt to virtue when they praise it.

MARLOW: True, madam; those who have most virtue in their mouths, have least of it in their bosoms. But I'm sure I tire you, madam.

MISS HARDCASTLE: Not in the least, Sir; there's something so agreeable and spirited in your manner, such life and force—pray, Sir, go on.

MARLOW: Yes, madam. I was saying—that there are some occasions—when a total want of courage, madam, destroys all the—and puts us—upon a—a—a—

MISS HARDCASTLE: I agree with you entirely, a want of courage upon some occasions assumes the appearance of ignorance, and betrays us when we most want to excel. I beg you'll proceed.

MARLOW: Yes, Madam. Morally speaking, madam—But I see Miss Neville expecting us in the next room. I would not intrude for the world.

MISS HARDCASTLE: I protest, Sir, I never was more agreeably entertained in all my life. Pray go on.

MARLOW: Yes, madam. I was—But she beckons us to join her. Madam, shall I do myself the honour to attend you?

MISS HARDCASTLE: Well then, I'll follow.

MARLOW (*aside*): This pretty smooth dialogue has done for me. [*Exit*]

MISS HARDCASTLE *sola*

MISS HARDCASTLE: Ha! ha! ha! Was there ever such a sober sentimental interview? I'm certain he scarce look'd in my face the whole time. Yet the fellow, but for his unaccountable bashfulness, is pretty well too. He has good sense, but then so buried in his fears, that it fatigues one more than ignorance. If I could teach him a little confidence, it would be doing somebody that I know of a piece of service. But who is that somebody?—that, faith, is a question I can scarce answer.   [*Exit.*]

In Kate's presence Marlow becomes a 'man of sensibility'; his emotions are open to her to such a degree that her slightest word or gesture can impinge on him, and the result of this, in his case, is to reduce him to social ineptitude.   These traits Goldsmith exploits in the encounter in Act 2.

There is something ironic in Hastings' remark at the beginning of the section that he is proud to bring 'two persons of such merit together, that only want to know, to esteem each other'. By the end of the section Kate believes Marlow to be bashful and 'buried in his fears' and Marlow who, because of his shyness scarcely looks at Kate, believes her to be squinting and over-serious. Yet Hastings speaks the truth, for Marlow and Kate, as the hero and heroine of the piece, are cut out for each other; the trials that separate them are only temporary ones.

Throughout the conversation Kate has to take the lead: she begins by referring to Marlow's accidents. The first to these was that Marlow and Hastings lost their way: the second, of which both parties are in ignorance, but not the audience, so that the words have an ironic undertone, is that Marlow has been deceived and believes he has arrived at an inn; and lastly, only moments before, Hastings has remarked that it was a fortuitous accident that Kate and Constance had arrived at the 'inn'. Marlow picks on the word 'accident' and haltingly tries to concoct a sentence around it, gaining encouragement from Hastings which the audience recognises as a hyperbole and further irony: 'You never spoke better in your life.' The audience has witnessed Marlow's loquacity at both 'The Three Pigeons' and on arrival at Hardcastle's house. Hastings' encouragement continues in the same vein, likening Marlow's rhetoric to Cicero's – a gross exaggeration. In this conversation Marlow is hardly accurate in describing himself as an observer of life. He is so unobservant that he fails to recognise Kate when he next meets her and, on his own admission, when present at the Ladies Club the 'agreeable Rattle' is obviously a partaker of life, rather than a detached surveyor of it.

Hastings and Constance *exeunt*, leaving Marlow and Kate to themselves. As Marlow becomes more nervous the register of his speech changes: the dialogue suggests that he has a patterned formal speech in mind which he is unable to deliver successfully. The failing he had earlier confessed to Hastings, that 'a single glance from a pair of fine eyes' overcame his ability to 'rattle away', is exemplified before the eyes of the audience. It is a characteristic of Goldsmith's technique as a playwright that the audience is frequently given information verbally and then it either witnesses the circumstances enacted or sees the result of these circumstances. In contrast the audience notes that Kate's speeches are well-modulated and that she is much in command of the situation, several times constructing Marlow's sentences for him.

Kate's asides to the auditorium probably involved moving away from Marlow, either towards the boxes or to the front of the stage, thus detaching herself momentarily from the action. The psychological effect of this on the audience is for Kate to engage the sympathy of its members, so that at the end of this section, when she makes her solo speech, there is a rapport between the actress and the spectators. Quite often the asides are an opportunity for a humorous remark, as with her second and Marlow's own two asides in this excerpt.

Kate is not above making ironic remarks at Marlow's expense. She tells him that there is 'something so agreeable and spirited' in his manner and asserts that she 'never was more agreeably entertained' by the conversation. Marlow is hardly to be taken in by these remarks and the audience certainly is not. Such barbs are a further clue to Kate's character: she possesses a plain common-sense attitude to the young man who is visiting her as a prospective husband, a contrast with his own over-sensitive reaction to her.

The excerpt finishes with a solo speech in which Kate summarises the effect of her meeting with Marlow, and leads the audience's expectation forward in her remark that in teaching the young man how to gain confidence she will be of service to someone – but who? This solo speech is also a happy method of linking the parody of the sentimental encounter, an incident of quiet amusement, with the broader humour of the encounter between Hastings, the authority on fashionable metropolitan taste, and Mrs Hardcastle, the country woman with a veneer of society manners.

6.3   A CONTRASTING ENCOUNTER

MISS HARDCASTLE: Never fear me. I think I have got the true bar cant.—Did your honour call?—Attend the Lion there.—Pipes and tobacco for the Angel.—The Lamb has been outrageous this half hour.

MAID: It will do, madam. But he's here.   [*Exit* MAID]

Enter MARLOW

MARLOW: What a bawling in every part of the house; I have scarce a
moment's repose. If I go to the best room, there I find my host
and his story. If I fly to the gallery, there we have my hostess
with her curtsey down to the ground. I have at last got a moment
to myself, and now for recollection. [*Walks and muses*]

MISS HARDCASTLE: Did you call, Sir? did your honour call?

MARLOW (*Musing*): As for Miss Hardcastle, she's too grave and sentimental for me.

MISS HARDCASTLE: Did your honour call?

[*She still places herself before him, he turning away*]

MARLOW: No, child (*musing*). Besides from the glimpse I had of her, I
think she squints.

MISS HARDCASTLE: I'm sure, Sir, I heard the bell ring.

MARLOW: No, no! (*musing*) I have pleased my father, however, by
coming down, and I'll to-morrow please myself by returning.

[*Taking out his tablets, and perusing*]

MISS HARDCASTLE: Perhaps the other gentleman called, Sir.

MARLOW: I tell you, no.

MISS HARDCASTLE: I should be glad to know, Sir. We have such a
parcel of servants.

MARLOW: No, no, I tell you. (*Looks full in her face*) Yes, child, I
think I did call. I wanted—I wanted—I vow, child, you are vastly
handsome.

MISS HARDCASTLE: O la, Sir, You'll make one asham'd.

MARLOW: Never saw a more sprightly malicious eye. Yes, yes, my
dear, I did call. Have you got any of your—a—what d'ye call it in
the house?

MISS HARDCASTLE: No, Sir, we have been out of that these ten days.

MARLOW: One may call in this house, I find, to very little purpose.
Suppose I should call for a taste, just by way of trial, of the nectar
of your lips; perhaps I might be disappointed in that too.

MISS HARDCASTLE: Nectar! nectar! that's a liquor there's no call for
in these parts. French, I suppose. We keep no French wines here,
Sir.

MARLOW: Of true English growth, I assure you.

MISS HARDCASTLE: Then it's odd I should not know it. We brew all
sorts of wines in this house, and I have lived here these eighteen
years.

MARLOW: Eighteen years! Why one would think, child, you kept the bar before you were born. How old are you?

MISS HARDCASTLE: O! Sir, I must not tell my age. They say women and music should never be dated.

MARLOW: To guess at this distance, you can't be much above forty (*approaching*.) Yet nearer I don't think so much (*approaching*.) By coming close to some women they look younger still; but when we come very close indeed (*attempting to kiss her*.)

MISS HARDCASTLE: Pray, Sir, keep your distance. One would think you wanted to know one's age as they do horses, by mark of mouth.

MARLOW: I protest, child, you use me extremely ill. If you keep me at this distance, how is it possible you and I can be ever acquainted?

MISS HARDCASTLE: And who wants to be acquainted with you? I want no such acquaintance, not I. I'm sure you did not treat Miss Hardcastle that was here awhile ago in this obstropalous manner. I'll warrant me, before her you look'd dash'd, and kept bowing to the ground, and talk'd, for all the world, as if you was before a justice of peace.

MARLOW (*Aside*): Egad! she has hit it, sure enough. (*To her*) In awe of her, child? Ha! ha! ha! A mere, awkward, squinting thing, no, no, I find you don't know me. I laugh'd, and rallied her a little; but I was unwilling to be too severe. No, I could not be too severe, *curse me*!

MISS HARDCASTLE: O! then, Sir, you are a favourite, I find, among the ladies?

MARLOW: Yes, my dear, a great favourite. And yet, hang me, I don't see what they find in me to follow. At the Ladies Club in town, I'm called their agreeable Rattle. Rattle, child, is not my real name, but one I'm known by. My name is Solomons. Mr. Solomons, my dear, at your service. (*Offering to salute her*)

MISS HARDCASTLE: Hold, Sir; you were introducing me to your club, not to yourself. And you're so great a favourite there you say?

MARLOW: Yes, my dear. There's Mrs Mantrap, Lady Betty Blackleg, the Countess of Sligo, Mrs Langhorns, old Miss Biddy Buckskin, and your humble servant, keep up the spirit of the place.

MISS HARDCASTLE: Then it's a very merry place, I suppose.

MARLOW: Yes, as merry as cards, suppers, wine, and old women can make us.

MISS HARDCASTLE: And their agreeable Rattle, ha! ha! ha!

MARLOW (*Aside*): Egad! I don't quite like this chit. She looks knowing, methinks. You laugh, child!

MISS HARDCASTLE: I can't but laugh to think what time they all have for minding their work or their family.

MARLOW (*Aside*): All's well, she don't laugh at me. (*To her*) Do *you* ever work, child?

MISS HARDCASTLE: Ay, sure. There's not a screen or a quilt in the whole house but what can bear witness to that.

MARLOW: Odso! Then you must shew me your embroidery. I embroider and draw patterns myself a little. If you want a judge of your work you must apply to me.   [*Seizing her hand*]

MISS HARDCASTLE: Ay, but the colours don't look well by candle light. You shall see in the morning.   [*Struggling*]

MARLOW: And why not now, my angel? Such beauty fires beyond the power of resistance.—Pshaw! the father here! My old luck: I never nick'd seven that I did not throw ames ace three times following.   [*Exit* MARLOW]

In the parallel interview in Act 3 the audience sees Kate preparing to assume a barmaid's role. She gives her reasons for playing this part: she wants to be noticed by Marlow as when she was presented in her own person Marlow was too shy to look at her; furthermore she wants to become acquainted with him, especially at a time when he is not on his guard. She then gives her imitation of the barmaid, calling for the requirements of people in the various rooms which she has imagined are named after animals instead of our present habit of numbering them. In making mention of the Lion and the Lamb she is possibly musing on Marlow's two contrasting approaches to women, whilst picturing herself as the Angel.

It is Kate who has to persist in making advances to Marlow - incidentally learning of his opinion of Miss Hardcastle who, he felt, is 'too grave and sentimental' for him. Kate, with her clear notions of what she wishes to achieve, and her forthright drive, can hardly be described as a woman of sentiment. There is a treble irony in this remark: Marlow not only fails to recognise Kate when he makes his opinion known; he also fails to recognise both her own, and indeed his own, basic characteristics; for it is he who in Act 2 was presented as the person of sentiment.

Marlow quickly changes from the preoccupied young man to the man of dalliance, plainly revealing this in the register of his language: no longer does he speak half of himself; instead he plays a verbal game with Kate: 'Have you got any of your — a — what d'ye call it in the house.' He starts to play the role of the flirter which matches her own masquerade as the maid. A game which Hastings and Mrs Hardcastle play, as well as Mrs Hardcastle and her husband, badinage about one's age, is engaged in by Marlow and Kate. Marlow's mistake about Kate's age is an opportunity for him to advance towards her physically. Kate has a down-to-earth, but witty, response. 'One would think you wanted to know one's age as they do horses, by mark of mouth.' Throughout the scene it is evident that she is in charge, manipulating Marlow.

In the following lines Goldsmith uses to the full the situation of mistaken identity, piling one ironical remark on another. In her disguise Kate is able to refer to Marlow's reaction to her true *persona*. He, for his part, speaks disparagingly of Kate, and comments on her supposed deficiencies of eyesight, whilst it is he himself who is blind and imperceptive.

Seemingly chance remarks in earlier scenes have given the audience the information that Marlow behaves like a rake once he is amongst women of the lower classes. Marlow earlier admitted to this himself; 'But among females of another class you know — ' And knowingly he tells Hardcastle: 'The girls like finery.'

In Act 3 Marlow gives a cameo of his social encounters at the Ladies Club, properly the Paphian Society, founded for social amusement and 'gallantry' but not, as Marlow half implies, for any kind of scandal. It was quite normal for gentlemen to be admitted to this club which was situated centrally in London in Albermarle Street. The list of members Marlow recites is one of monied and titled ladies, amongst whom Marlow is supposed to be reticent, so possibly Goldsmith intended the description to be a figment of Marlow's imagination. 'Biddy Buckskin' replaces an over-obvious reference to Rachael Lloyd, one of the founders of the club. The 'old women' are not, of course, presented in a very flattering light.

Marlow has already made one advance towards Kate and attempted to kiss her; the latter part of the encounter is another bold move on his part, as he attempts to take Kate to the bedroom to examine her embroidery. This ploy is foiled by the sudden appearance of Hardcastle. A hint of prescience is given in Kate's remark that Marlow will 'see all in the morning'. That is the time when the mistaken identities are explained and the complexities of the night unravelled. Marlow's final metaphor is from dicing – to 'nick seven' was to throw a six and a one and an 'ames ace' consisted of a double one.

In the two incidents Goldsmith allows the audience to see the two contradictory natures of Marlow in confrontation. He has carefully prepared the spectators for this by verbal reference to Marlow's behaviour. Thus much of the humour in the scene is obtained from the audience watching its prior expectations realised in the action, which makes for entertaining theatre. Goldsmith views Marlow's diverse behaviour as a 'folly'; in order to highlight this and make it thoroughly ridiculous he exaggerates the folly. Thus he is taking a satirical look at an instance of human behaviour. However, in so doing, Goldsmith realises that he is open to censure by the critics of his day, for, he wrote: '. . . they have prescribed the comic or satyrical muse from every walk but high life, which, though abounding in fools as well as the humblest station, is by no means so fruitful in adversity.'

7 THE CRITICAL RECEPTION

7.1 THE FIRST PERFORMANCE

Until the day before the first performance it had been assumed that his play was to be known by Goldsmith's original title, 'The Mistakes of a Night'. The playwright was unhappy with this and his friends, according to Dr Johnson, had been 'in labour' to find a more suitable title, but without success. Some trial had been made with *The Novel*, a reference to Tony Lumpkin's fiction about Hardcastle's house but this title did not offer a pithy summary of the plot of the complete play. In one of her speeches Kate declares that she will retain her disguise in which she has 'Stoop'd to conquer' Marlow, and the phrase was seized on in Goldsmith's hurriedly penned epilogue:

Well, having stoop'd to conquer with success . . .

It was this which led to the new title for the play. The playbills had been published and at once the order was sent by the stage manager for *The Mistakes of a Night* to be superseded by *She Stoops to Conquer*.

Friends of Goldsmith attended the first night in force. Dr Johnson was present, as was Sir Joshua Reynolds, the founder-president of the Royal Academy, and Richard Cumberland the playwright. In his biography Richard Cumberland states that many eyes were on Johnson, sitting in a side box, and when this arbiter of taste laughed, members of the audience felt safe in roaring their delight too. Goldsmith was fearful for his creation and spent the evening walking in St James' Park until near the end of the play when he crept into one of the boxes. His fears

were groundless; the response of the audience was a lively and enthusiastic one.

7.2 THE CRITICAL RESPONSE

Accolade

Newspaper critics, too, greeted the play with approval. The *Morning Chronicle* noted that Goldsmith had departed from the conventions of the sentimental comedy, and voiced its approval accordingly.

The critic commented on the characters which Goldsmith had created. He found Hardcastle a 'good-natured particular old fellow' who as the father capable of being ridiculed was a suitable subject for comedy; but the drawing was balanced for his farcical characteristics did not cause embarrassment. Marlow, he thought, was an original character – he did not descend from a lineage of stage characters as did both Hardcastle and Lumpkin. Furthermore the writer found Marlow's varying response to women to be a completely credible one, a belief which possibly eludes us now. Nor did he think Tony Lumpkin exceeded credibility. The writer itemised that character's three principal characteristics: he was made up of 'whim and good-natured mischief'; he was the means by which the plot was advanced; and he was the source of much of the amusement in the play.

Censure

This enthusiastic response to the play must be balanced by a minority reaction. Horace Walpole, an author and letter-writer of the period, may stand for those who found the humour, with its stress on the antics and caroussings of the rustics, low. He wrote to his friend, the Revd William Mason:

> The drift tends to no moral, no edification of any kind. The situations, however, are well imagined, and make one laugh, in spite of the grossness of the dialogue, the forced witticisms, and total improbability of the whole plan and conduct. But what disgusts me most is, that though the characters are very low, and aim at low humour, not one of them says a sentence that is natural or marks any character at all. It is set up in opposition to sentimental comedy, and is as bad as the worst of them.

There is no reconciling the conflicting responses of the reviewer in the *Morning Chronicle* and of Sir Horace Walpole. Walpole's response is a result of conservatism. Shaped by traditional eighteenth-century canons of taste he finds difficulty in accepting some of the characters, the plot and the dialogue. He is blind to Goldsmith's wit and sees only comical situations: he realises the play is a reaction against sentimental comedy, but he cannot appreciate *She Stoops to Conquer* as a replacement for it. The newspaper reviewer is more liberal in his acceptances: he is willing to take the comedy as Goldsmith presents it, freed from the older conventions which by 1773 had grown stale.

Dr Johnson was constantly breaking away from the shackles of taste. His own response to *She Stoops to Conquer* was highly enthusiastic and he realised Goldsmith's prime intention in writing the play. It was more than a refutation of the sentimental drama; it was an essay in laughter:

> I know of no comedy for many years that has so exhilarated an audience, that has answered so much the great end of comedy making an audience merry.

7.3 ESTABLISHMENT IN THE REPERTOIRE

In its first season, from March until the end of May, *She Stoops to Conquer* received twelve performances. Some of these were benefit performances for the author of the piece, and from them Goldsmith reaped a reward of £502.18.6d. The popularity of the play rapidly spread geographically and during 1773 performances were given in Paris, Dublin, the theatre in John Street, New York, as well as in many Georgian playhouses throughout England. Subsequently the play passed into the repertoire of the English theatre. From the beginning of the nineteenth century *She Stoops to Conquer* enjoyed occasional revivals in the provinces, but it rarely appeared on the London stage. Its other provenance was as the school play; possibly it was thought to be suitable for young stagers because of its absence of marital problems and moral impropriety. The National Theatre Company mounted the play at the Lyttleton Theatre in November 1984, following a tour of the provinces. In fact the opening night of the revival was given at the delightful Theatre Royal in Bath.

7.4   THE REVIVAL AT THE NATIONAL THEATRE

Design

Sets and costumes were designed by Alison Chitty. As spectators entered the auditorium they saw that a painted *rideau* hid the set from sight: it depicted the hill on which the Hardcastles' house was set, but without giving any geographical identity. The same lack of decision about the location became evident when the drop cloth was drawn up to reveal the chamber of the house. A heavy chimney breast, under which a fire burnt, formed the focal point of a truncated long room. This device allowed the audience to feel as though its members were sitting within the chamber, sharing the life of the Hardcastle family. Thus the same intimacy was afforded as in the Georgian theatre. This sense of proximity is important, so that the characters' asides to the audience may be made as simply as by a turn of the head. Rapid changes of scene were possible as the chimney was mounted on a revolve which, when turned, brought to the fore the scenes set in 'The Three Pigeons' and at the end of the garden. For the latter scene the revolve was pushed upstage, so making room for a spreading tree, previously half concealed, to be pushed into full view towards the front of the stage. Together with the rising mists and the darkness the representation, consisting only of a section of the house and the tree, suggested economically the atmosphere of a night in which danger lurked. By means of the revolve, scene changes could be made rapidly. Furniture that needed moving was shifted by the household servants.

Numbers of critics spoke of the glowing warmth of the play and for this quality the setting must be commended.

The Performers

The casting supervisor was able to draw into this production a number of actors who had firmly established themselves through television and variety as well as in the conventional theatre. In this he held an advantage over Goldsmith, for the eighteenth-century performers whom he would have chosen declined his invitation to appear in the comedy, fearful that George Colman's premonition would be realised and the play fail at its opening night.

As Tony Lumpkin Tony Haygarth gave a highly inventive, noisy performance, blowing his bugle through the corridors of the rumbling mansion; and yet, as the play progressed, he revealed a guileless like-ability and worked his way into the secure affections of the audience. Touches of humour peppered his playing: when his pipe needed cleaning he simply knocked the dead tobacco out onto his cousin's décolletage. Michael Billington observed in the *Guardian* (10 November 1984), the extent to which 'his thirst for revenge on the Hardcastle house stems from the fact that he has been deprived of his birthright and reared like a household pet'. The forceful self-interest with which Lumpkin insti-gated the plot was, as the play progressed, visibly subdued by his upsurging *bonhomie*.

Dora Bryan built the role of Mrs Hardcastle on a clear concept: '. . . to me she seems a really pushy woman, you know the kind, dying to ascend the social ladder' (quoted in *What's On*, 1 November 1984). However, in her protrayal Miss Bryan was in danger of forgetting that Mrs Hardcastle was the prior established hierarchical figure in the village at the time of her first marriage; if anyone were to climb a social ladder it would be her husband, Hardcastle, who had married into her property. The role was effectively shared with the audience, often by a move downstage to speak directly to the auditorium, thus illustrating the extent to which an eighteenth-century playwright thought of the spectators as a factor in his play.

Hardcastle was presented by Tom Baker as an unpompous duffer of a man; yet in watching his nervous mannerisms, his eager runs about the stage, one realised how he had learnt to use his idiosyncracies to become the survivor of a marriage to Mrs Hardcastle. If he could remain afloat over the years of that marriage, then nothing Marlow could do in the course of an evening would floor him.

The part of Marlow was given a muted performance by Hywel Bennett. Throughout, he appeared stiffened by worrying over the problems of travel and society, and yet the mannerisms which Goldsmith suggested belonged to the character – a stammer, short sightedness, an ability to become the 'agreeable Rattle' – were not taken up. Malcolm Kay wrote in the *Observer* (11 November 1984) of Bennett's

> inability to convey Marlow's tongue-tied embarrassment at wooing Hardcastle's daughter. It is a small point but a vital one: Marlow's peculiarly English sexual proclivities . . . is lacking the most crucial element.

Of the two young travellers it was left to Gregory Floy to portray Hastings as a balance of artifice and feeling; this skilful marriage of manner and emotion defeated Kate and Constance, played by Julia Watson and Kelly Hunter, and so they gave performances which lost out on style.

Direction

It is the director's task to envisage the play as a harmonious unity and thus to shape the designers', musicians' and actors' offerings into a coherent performance on the stage. Giles Block, who directed this revival, began by steeping himself in an understanding of Goldsmith's life and times. He told Christopher Warman in an interview for *The Times* (3 November 1984):

> ... I settled down to read all [Goldsmith's] works and about his life, and the more I read the more I realised that the play was about his early life. There is a lot of Goldsmith in Tony Lumpkin and Marlow, and the relationships of the characters recall those of his own family.

Perhaps it was this realisation of the play as a close-knit, family affair which helped the ensuing presentation to generate good nature and homely humour. The story was told with a commendable directness and simplicity which, one felt, was totally in key with Goldsmith's writing. Of course, the director might have chosen other routes in his interpretation of the text, and in an illuminating review (*The Times*, 10 November 1984) Irving Wardle jotted down some of the choices which confront one:

> Just how debauched is young Marlow? And how far does he go with Kate in her barmaid masquerade? What marital hatred may be lurking under the Hardcastles' squabbles; and what might Tony be getting up to down the garden with Bet Bouncer?

The summation of Block's response to the spirit of the play was seen in the last episode, set around the family table laden with good things to eat: it was the supper so long delayed by thwarted elopement and punitive journeyings. In grosser plots and novels eating was a sign of sexual consumption; but in this sunny production it was a happy anticipation of the wedded life of the two young couples whose fortunes had been traced through the course of an evening.

REVISION QUESTIONS

Each of the following revision questions is intended to redirect students to the text of *She Stoops to Conquer*. Quite often the question will suggest an idea which you need to trace through several scenes or through the whole play. Make notes of these threads of references, not forgetting to include a reminder to yourself of where a particular reference occurs in the play. It is advisable to make a skeleton answer in note form from your initial jottings and from this to write the final answer. If time is short, it is more valuable to compose a number of skeleton answers than to attempt only a limited number of finished answers.

1. Account for the longevity on the stage of *She Stoops to Conquer* when other eighteenth-century plays are now forgotten.
2. To what effect does Goldsmith use disguise and mistaken identity in *She Stoops to Conquer*?
3. Is Marlow, Hastings or Lumpkin the true hero of the play?
4. Compare and contrast the characters of the two pairs of lovers in *She Stoops to Conquer*.
5. Does Kate or Hardcastle have the truer estimate of Marlow's character?
6. To what extent is *She Stoops to Conquer* an essay on Marlow's self-discovery?
7. How does Goldsmith use stock comic devices to advance the plot of his play?
8. In spite of his dislike of sentimental comedy, did Goldsmith in reality write one in *She Stoops to Conquer*?

9. If you were designing a production of *She Stoops to Conquer* what setting would you devise?

10. Do the minor characters in *She Stoops to Conquer* have any real part in the plot?

11. What facets of Georgian life does Goldsmith present to his audience in *She Stoops to Conquer*?

12. Comment on Horace Walpole's criticism of *She Stoops to Conquer*: '. . . it is not the subject I condemn, though very vulgar, but the execution. The drift tends to no moral, no edification of any kind'.

13. 'The English seem to us to have excelled . . . in the strength of their characters, the warmth and bustle of their plots, and the variety of their incidents'. Examine *She Stoops to Conquer* in the light of this claim.

14. '. . . when [Goldsmith] has thrust his people into a situation, he makes them talk very *funnily*.' Illustrate and comment on this contemporary critic's remark.

15. Write a review of a production of *She Stoops to Conquer* which you have seen, bearing in mind Goldsmith's intentions in writing the play.

FURTHER READING

9.1 WORKS BY OLIVER GOLDSMITH

The Collected Works of Oliver Goldsmith, ed. Arthur Friedman (Oxford: Clarendon Press, 1966). Goldsmith's works complete in five volumes. There is a full introduction to each of his writings, as well as copious footnotes. This collected edition is invaluable for reference purposes.

Plays and Poems, ed. Tom Davis (London. Dent, 1975). The Introduction gives a useful survey of Goldsmith's two plays and the more important of his poems.

9.2 LITERARY AND HISTORICAL BACKGROUND, CRITICISM AND BIOGRAPHY

Balderston, Katherine A. (ed.), *The Collected Letters of Oliver Goldsmith* (Cambridge University Press, 1928). In addition to the letters this little book contains an important section on the first production of *She Stoops to Conquer*, as well as Mrs Hodson's brief memoirs of her brother.

Ginger, John, *The Notable Man* (London: Hamish Hamilton, 1977). An authoritative biography of Goldsmith.

Goldsmith: The Critical Heritage, ed. G. S. Rousseau (London: Routledge, 1974). Contemporary reviews of stage performances and of the publication of *She Stoops to Conquer* are given.

Jeffares, A. Norman, *Oliver Goldsmith* (London: Longman, 1959, revised 1965). A brief survey of Goldsmith's life and writings in the British Council's series, *Writers and their Work*.

Novak, Maximillian E., *Eighteenth-Century English Literature* (London: Macmillan, 1983). A useful survey, with the help of which Goldsmith may be placed in his literary context.

Porter, Roy, *English Society in the Eighteenth Century* (London: Penguin, 1982).

The Revels History of Drama in English, Volume VI: 1750–1880, ed. Clifford Leech and T. W. Craik, (London: Metheun, 1975). This illustrated work describes in detail the theatrical conditions that prevailed in Goldsmith's day. A copious bibliography is given.

Reynolds, Joshua, *Portraits*, ed. Frederick W. Hilles (London: Heinemann, 1952). A brief life of Goldsmith by his contemporary and friend.

Sells, A. Lytton, *Oliver Goldsmith. His Life and Works* (London: Allen & Unwin, 1974). A comprehensive critical biography.

Sherbo, Arthur, *English Sentimental Drama* (East Lansing: Michigan State University Press, 1957). Although the references to Goldsmith are in passing, this study relates Goldsmith's comedies to the prevailing literary tastes.

Trevelyan, G. M., *Illustrated English Social History: III* (London; Penguin, 1964, reprinted 1966). The eighteenth-century background to Goldsmith's life and writing.

MACMILLAN STUDENTS' NOVELS

General Editor: JAMES GIBSON

The Macmillan Students' Novels are low-priced, new editions of major classics, aimed at the first examination candidate. Each volume contains:

* enough explanation and background material to make the novels accessible – and rewarding to pupils with little or no previous knowledge of the author or the literary period;

* detailed notes elucidate matters of vocabulary, interpretation and historical background;

* eight pages of plates comprising facsimiles of manuscripts and early editions, portraits of the author and photographs of the geographical setting of the novels.

JANE AUSTEN: MANSFIELD PARK
Editor: Richard Wirdnam

JANE AUSTEN: NORTHANGER ABBEY
Editor: Raymond Wilson

JANE AUSTEN: PRIDE AND PREJUDICE
Editor: Raymond Wilson

JANE AUSTEN: SENSE AND SENSIBILITY
Editor: Raymond Wilson

JANE AUSTEN: PERSUASION
Editor: Richard Wirdnam

CHARLOTTE BRONTË: JANE EYRE
Editor: F. B. Pinion

EMILY BRONTË: WUTHERING HEIGHTS
Editor: Graham Handley

JOSEPH CONRAD: LORD JIM
Editor: Peter Hollindale

CHARLES DICKENS: GREAT EXPECTATIONS
Editor: James Gibson

CHARLES DICKENS: HARD TIMES
Editor: James Gibson

CHARLES DICKENS: OLIVER TWIST
Editor: Guy Williams

CHARLES DICKENS: A TALE OF TWO CITIES
Editor: James Gibson

GEORGE ELIOT: SILAS MARNER
Editor: Norman Howlings

GEORGE ELIOT: THE MILL ON THE FLOSS
Editor: Graham Handley

D. H. LAWRENCE: SONS AND LOVERS
Editor: James Gibson

D. H. LAWRENCE: THE RAINBOW
Editor: James Gibson

MARK TWAIN: HUCKLEBERRY FINN
Editor: Christopher Parry